Messenger

Messenger

New and Selected Poems
1976 – 2006

Ellen Bryant Voigt

W. W. NORTON & COMPANY

NEW YORK   LONDON

Ellen Bryant Voigt, "The Hen," "Harvest," "Dialogue Poetics," "Stork," "Damage," "The Letter," "The Visit," "Snakeskin," and "Tropics" from *Claiming Kin* © 1976 by Ellen Bryant Voigt and reprinted by permission of Wesleyan University Press.

For information about permission to reproduce selections from this book, write to Permissions, W. W. Norton & Company, Inc., 500 Fifth Avenue, New York, NY 10110

Manufacturing by The Courier Companies, Inc.
Book design by Brooke Koven
Production manager: Andrew Marasia

Library of Congress Cataloging-in-Publication Data

Voigt, Ellen Bryant, date.
Messenger : new and selected poems, 1976–
2006 / Ellen Bryant Voigt. —1st ed.
p. cm.
ISBN-13: 978-0-393-06250-2
ISBN-10: 0-393-06250-3
I. Title.
PS3572.O34M47 2007
811'.54—dc22
2006024613

W. W. Norton & Company, Inc., 500 Fifth Avenue, New York, N.Y. 10110
www.wwnorton.com

W. W. Norton & Company Ltd., Castle House, 75/76 Wells Street, London W1T 3QT

1 2 3 4 5 6 7 8 9 0

Francis

Contents

FROM *The Lotus Flowers* (1987)

Messenger: New Poems (2006)

Acknowledgments

The new poems first appeared in *The American Poetry Review*, *The Atlantic*, *Blackbird*, *The Kenyon Review*, *The New England Review*, and *TriQuarterly*. "The Feeder" was reprinted in *The Pushcart Prize* (vol. xxx) and "Harvesting the Cows" in *The Best American Poetry 2005*. Thanks to these editors.

Thanks to the Rockefeller Foundation for a month's stay at Bellagio; to the Academy of American Poets for its James Merrill Fellowship; and, at W. W. Norton, to Amy Cherry, David Stanford Burr, and Carol Houck Smith, who has brought so much poetry to the world.

I want also to acknowledge poets whose work prompted or enabled some of these poems. In earlier books, Stephen Dobyns (the narratives in *The Lotus Flowers*), William Meredith ("Effort at Speech"), Allen Grossman ("Song and Story"), and Agha Shahid Ali ("Himalaya"). In this one, Reg Gibbons and Michael Ryan ("Rubato"), Carl Phillips ("Redbud"), and Michael Collier ("The Feeder").

Finally, my deep gratitude for the acute, candid, instructive responses I have received from generous readers over the years, too many to be listed here; from my canny newest reader, James Longenbach; from my first reader, my touchstone, Louise Glück.

from ❧

CLAIMING KIN

1976

THE HEN

The neck lodged under a stick,
the stick under her foot,
she held the full white breast
with both hands, yanked up and out,
and the head was delivered of the body.
Brain stuck like a lens; the profile
fringed with red feathers.
Deposed, abstracted,
the head lay on the ground like a coin.
But the rest, released into the yard,
language and direction wrung from it,
flapped the insufficient wings
and staggered forward, convulsed, instinctive—
I thought it was sobbing to see it hump the dust,
pulsing out those muddy juices,
as if something, deep in the gizzard,
in the sack of soft nuggets,
drove it toward the amputated member.
Even then, watching it litter the ground
with snowy refusals, I knew it was this
that held life, gave life,
and not the head with its hard contemplative eye.

HARVEST

The farmer circles the pasture
checking fences. Deep
in the broomstraw, the dove withholds

her three notes. The sky
to the southwest is uniformly
blue. Years of plowing under

have brought this red clay to its
green conclusion.
Down back,

the herd
clusters to the loading pen.
Only disease or dogpack

could alter such order. Is that
what he asks for in the late
fields, the falling afternoon?

DIALOGUE: POETICS

1st Voice

Admiring the web, do we
forget the spider? The real
poem is a knife-edge,
quick and clean.

The bird needs
no extra feather, the stone
sits in its own shape.

Consider the weather.

We could say that snow
fills the crotches of the birch
and makes a webbed hand.

We could say,
Look at the graceful line
of falling snow!

The point is: It
falls and falls on trees
and houses, with or
without comment.

2nd Voice

ITEM:
Should we record snow
falling on the tamaracks
beside the black Winooski
River, and not the trapper
crouched on the far bank,
who thinks: Such
silence, such order.

ITEM:
Seven stones in a circle make
eight shapes.

ITEM:
Not being birds, we seek our own
windpatterns, fashion
the lute, discover language.

ITEM:
Following the taut strands
that span flower and drainspout,
down the long loops, moving
through the spider's whole house,
we come round to the center
and the patient jewel in its own setting.

STORK

There are seventeen species of stork.

The painted stork is pink in his nuptial plumage.

The milky stork woos with his large flat bill.

The marabou offers her carrion, as does the adjutant.

Due to irregular throat structure, storks have no voice;

they strike their beaks together in lovesong.

Newborns know to swallow the fish headfirst.

In the myth of the moon-bird, storks impregnate women.

All storks adhere to serial monogamy.

In the mating season, two species are migratory:

the black stork who roosts in platforms in the forests of Poland;

the familiar white stork ("good luck" in Western Europe).

They are surpassed in endurance by none but the arctic tern.

They travel a thousand miles to Africa.

They soar on the thermal current.

They precede the rainy season.

They carry the unborn in from the marshland.

If a stork nests in your chimney, a son will be born.

If a stork nests in your chimney, your house will be empty.

If a stork leaves the nest, that is an omen.

If a stork leaves the nest forever, disaster will strike the area.

If a stork's shadow falls on the rosebush, grief descends to the village.

If a stork is damaged, the weather darkens.

If you kill a stork, kinsmen surround you, clacking long sticks together
     like knives.

DAMAGE

It didn't suckle. That
was the first indication.

Looking back, I know how much I knew.
The repetitious bloodfall,

the grating at the door of bone,
the afterbirth stuck in my womb like a scab.

Others were lucky,
response was taken from them.

Each time I bathe him
in his little tub, I think

How easy to let go

Let go

THE LETTER

She sits at the table
with her small collection of treasure.
Chooses from it a shell whose delicate edges whorl
inward to a palm, a lifeprint.
Inside this pastel saucer,
parsley and chives recall a Japanese garden:
clean, immutable.
If only she were there,
a single tiny figure by the pool,
holding the letter.
If only she were rock, tree, clear water.

THE VISIT

The afternoon spreads its fingers on the lawn,
and such light as penetrates the shrubs
enters the house with hesitation.
I have come from a great distance
to find my father asleep in his large brown chair.
Why isn't he out in the fields, our common passion?
I want to wake him with kisses,
I want to reach out and stroke his hand.
But I turn away, without speech or gesture,
having for so long withheld my body from him.

SNAKESKIN

Down on the porch, the blacksnake
sits like a thick fist.
His back is flexed and slick.
The wedge of his forehead turns
to the sun. He does not remember
the skin shucked in the attic,
the high branches of our family tree.

The moth will not recall the flannel
cocoon. The snail empties the endless
convolutions of its shell. Think
of the husk of the locust,
sewn like an ear to the elm.
How easily they leave old lives,
as an eager lover steps from the skirts
at her ankles.   Sleep corrects memory:
the long sleep of bear and woodchuck,
the sleep of the sea,
the sleep of the wooden spool unwinding,
the sleep of snow, when houses lose
their angles and edges, the slow
sleep of no dreaming;
and we could rise up in new skins
to a full confusion of green,

to the slick stalks of grasses,
and the catalpa, that beany tree, offering
its great, white, aromatic promise.

TROPICS

In the still morning when you move
toward me in sleep, for love,
I dream of

an island where long-stemmed cranes,
serious weather vanes,
turn slowly on one

foot. There the dragonfly folds
his mica wings and rides
the tall reed

close as a handle. The hippo yawns,
nods to thick pythons,
slack and drowsy, who droop down

like untied sashes
from the trees. The brash
hyenas do not cackle

and run but lie with their paws
on their heads like dogs.
The lazy crow's caw

falls like a sigh. In the field
below, the fat moles build
their dull passage with an old

instinct that needs
no light or waking; its slow beat
turns the hand in sleep

as we turn toward each other
in the ripe air of summer,
before the change of weather,

before the heavy drop
of the apples.

from ❧

THE FORCES OF
PLENTY

1983

BLUE RIDGE

Up there on the mountain road, the fireworks
blistered and subsided, for once at eye level:
spatter of light like water flicked from the fingers;
the brief emergent pattern; and after the afterimage bled
from the night sky, a delayed and muffled thud
that must have seemed enormous down below,
the sound concomitant with the arranged
threat of fire above the bleachers.
I stood as tall and straight as possible,
trying to compensate, trying not to lean in my friend's
direction. Beside me, correcting height, he slouched
his shoulders, knees locked, one leg stuck out
to form a defensive angle with the other.
Thus we were most approximate
and most removed.
                    In the long pauses
between explosions, he'd signal conversation
by nodding vaguely toward the ragged pines.
I said my children would have loved the show.
He said we were watching youth at a great distance,
and I thought how the young
are truly boring, unvaried as they are
by the deep scar of doubt, the constant afterimage
of regret—no major tension in their bodies, no tender
hesitation, they don't yet know
that this is so much work, scraping

from the self its multiple desires; don't yet know
fatigue with self, the hunger for obliteration
that wakes us in the night at the dead hour
and fuels good sex.
                          Of course I didn't say it.
I realized he watched the fireworks
with the cool attention he had turned on women
dancing in the bar, a blunt uninvested gaze
calibrating every moving part, thighs,
breasts, the muscles of abandon.
I had wanted that gaze on me.
And as the evening dwindled to its nub,
its puddle of tallow, appetite without object,
as the men peeled off to seek
the least encumbered consolation
and the women grew expansive with regard—
how have I managed so long to stand among the paired
bodies, the raw pulsing music driving
loneliness into the air like scent,
and not be seized by longing,
not give anything to be summoned
into the larger soul two souls can make?
Watching the fireworks with my friend,
so little ease between us,
I see that I have armed myself;
fire changes everything it touches.

Perhaps he has foreseen this impediment.
Perhaps when he holds himself within himself,
a sheathed angular figure at my shoulder,
he means to be protective less of him
than me, keeping his complicating rage
inside his body. And what would it solve
if he took one hand from his pocket,
risking touch, risking invitation—
if he took my hand it would not alter
this explicit sadness.
                        The evening stalls,
the fireworks grow boring at this remove.
The traffic prowling the highway at our backs,
the couples, the families scuffling on the bank
must think us strangers to each other. Or,
more likely, with the celebrated fireworks thrusting
their brilliant repeating designs above the ridge,
we simply blur into the foreground,
like the fireflies dragging among the trees
their separate, discontinuous lanterns.

A FUGUE

I.

The body, a resonant bowl:
the irreducible gist of wood,
that memorized the turns
of increase and relinquishing:
the held silence
where formal music will be quarried
by the cry of the strings,
the cry of the mind,
under the rosined bow.

2.

The deaf listen
with compensatory hands,
touching the instrument.
Musicians also
listen, and speak, with their hands.

Such elemental implements.
The eye trains on a grid of ink,
and the fingers quicken,
habitual, learnéd,
to recover the arterial melody.

3.

The long habit of living
indisposes us to dying.
In this measured space,
a drastic weeping.

    *

Music depends
on its own diminishing.
Like the remembered dead,
roused from silence
and duplicated, the song heard
is sound leaving the ear.

    *

Medicine too is a temporal art.
Each day, children
are rendered into your keeping.
And so you take up your instruments
to make whole, to make live,
what others made.

4.

Pure science:
the cello in your lap;
the firm misleading bodies
of your own children
in your brother's room.
His illness is adult, and lethal.
You place the bow
and Beethoven turns again
from the stern physician
to annotate the page:
cantabile—
          meaning
not birdsong, windsong,
wind in the flue, bell, branch,
but the human voice,
distinct and perishable.

And you play for him.

THE HAPPINESS POEMS

A small figure going up the mountain—
not really a mountain, but a cliff,
a fist of rock carved first by the river,
then by the highway, and now patched
with brush and trees. Here and there
a birch among the evergreens,
and the steady red jacket like a flag.
Surely no one could break a trail
straight up, carrying groceries—
but from here at the Amoco
someone climbs through birch and hemlock,
carrying home two large brown bags,
someone takes a shortcut
straight up the side of a mountain.

     *

If there could be jubilation in the world!
The snow-draped south field
numbers four puddles of brown grass,
it's spring, there are healthy children
in the neighborhood, the lilac beginning—

     *

She lost them all,
and she is someone who knows someone I know.
I try to be happy,
warming outside like a shrub,
until the siren duplicates
that cry that stops the blood.
I want to be happy
in my small unsheltered garden,
my husband a stalk in the wind's teeth,
and our two seasonal blossoms,
one Sweet William,
one delicate wood anemone.

TALKING THE FIRE OUT

I.

The stanchioned cows behind him,
the assembled odors,
the dwindling closets of hay—

A farmer stands at the door of the barn:
When to plant, when to harvest:

he studies the remedial clouds,
the rehearsed fields,
red, ridged, and the air
palpable with rain.

2.

In that latitude, *come look*
might mean the long bellpull
swaying from a rafter of the barn—two snakes
mating, blacksnakes, barn snakes,
a farmer's charm;

                might mean
bring a chair to the field and watch
a king snake, wrapped around a moccasin,
squeezing it like a stopped heart,
finally unwind, unhinge its jaws
and swallow the jeweled head,
the rest of it shuddering in all day
until the king sidles down the furrow
with an extra tongue.

                   Nothing is learned
by turning away. Indian summer,
when we harvested the deathweed
or cut and bound the yellow loaves of hay,
the boys brought every species
to the ninth-grade lab—king snake,
blacksnake, copperhead, cottonmouth—
and jar after jar of hazardous yield
struck at the glass.

3.

My father in the doorway
with his usual semaphore—

why is it always the same gesture
for *hello* and *goodbye*?
He keeps his elbow tucked,
like a cop,
or does he only want to ask a question?

Away from home,
I take it as a blessing,
the vertical forearm,
the seamed, outfacing palm.

4.

If you have a call,
you cradle the injured limb
and lean over the burn
as though kneeling,

but do you talk to the flesh,
to provoke its deep revulsion?
or must you sing directly
to the fire, soothing the beast
of the fire, calling it
out of the hand,
                    a poultice of words
drawing off the sultry residue
until the flush recedes,
leaving original flesh,
no blister, no scar.

5.

Who can distinguish knowledge
from belief? Against
the dangers in your own house,
you take up every weapon—
                              Listen:
my father killed a copperhead
with a switch. Out fishing,
coming on it by the pond, knowing
the exact angle and trusting it,
he flicked the weed against its back
as he had often cast his lean line
over secretive waters.

6.

Nothing is learned by turning away,
nothing surmounted.

Scattering its wise colors everywhere,
over the red barn, the red fields,
the sun is going down,
and due east, parallel on the horizon,
one of its children up-
rising catches the light
in a round bucket,

as I bend to my work,
crooning over the hurt bodies,
muttering on the page.

FOR MY FATHER

1. Elegy

Turning from a loss,
as if turning from an open window,
its local composition:
limbs juxtaposed against the sky,
juncture of sky and hillock,
the stark debrided tree.

Autumn, and the shucked leaves
are eating *green*, absorbing it
even as they are severed or detaching—
red is what red leaves repel. Any abstraction
names a consequence.

He is not here
He is not here

Halfway through a life, seeing leaves
the color of fire and of wounds
swaddle the base of the broad
deciduous tree,
you turn from the window's

slice of terrible radiance
to face the cluttered interior on which it falls.

2. Pittsylvania County

In the front yard, my father and his son
are playing ball, the round egg arcs
toward a lap of brown leather, the sound
of an axe on green wood, a bass
hitting the water. The boy
could do this forever—only one glove
between them and he has it—the fireflies
already discernible on the hillside,
the grass wet, he doesn't falter
as he skirts the waist-high crabapple tree
or backs across the graveled drive.
What am I after? Not shagging flies
on the lawn with my father, and not
drying the last dish with a fresh towel.
My father is a stationary target
through increasing dark, and out from my brother's
cocked proficient arm, the ball leaps,
of its own volition, into his hand.

3. New England Graveyard

It is a foreign symmetry, unlike anything
in the earth's surface rubble—
the headstones grouped by family
to organize the sacred rows; the flowers
at the fresh site
forced blooms with exposed
glands of pollen and the widest throats;
even the neat packages
of food, each container marked
with the names of the living.
If there is a life beyond the body,
I think we have no use for order
but are buoyed past our individuating fear,
and that memory is not,
as now, a footprint filling with water.

YEAR'S END

The fingers lie in the lap,
separate, lonely, as in the field
the separate blades of grass
shrivel or grow tall.

We sat together in the little room,
the walls blotched with steam,
holding the baby as if the two of us
could breathe for him and were not helpless.
Upstairs, his sister turned in her sleep
as the phone rang—

to have wakened to a child's cry,
gagged and desperate,
and then repeat that terror when the call
split the quiet house and centered
its dire message:
                    a child was dead
and his mother so wrung by grief
she stared and stared
at the moon on its black stalk,
the road glistening like wire.
Rubbing the window clear of steam
as a child rubs sleep from its eyes,
and looking past the fence to where
he had plunged the sled up and down the hill,

we could still see the holes his feet made,
a staggered row of graves
extracting darkness from the snow.

When morning brought the new year in,
the fever broke, and fresh snow
bandaged the tracks on the hill.
For a long time we stayed in the room,
listening to him breathe,
like refugees who listen to the sea,
unable to fully rejoice, or fully grieve.

LIEBESGEDICHT

I love you as my other self, as the other
self of the tree is not the pale tree
in the flat hand of the river, but the earth
that holds, is held by, the root of the tree.
This is how the earth loves the river,
and why its least fold solicits each
impulsive stream until the gathered water
makes of earth a passage to the sea.

I'd like to draw a lesson from this figure,
and find some comfort in the way the larger
world rings with such dependencies.
But if I see ourselves in earth and water,
I also see one taken from the other,
the rivening wind loosed against the tree.

JUG BROOK

Beyond the stone wall,
the deer should be emerging from their yard.
Lank, exhausted, they scrape at the ground
where roots and bulbs will send forth
new definitions. The creek swells in its ditch;
the field puts on a green glove.
Deep in the woods, the dead ripen,
and the lesser creatures turn to their commission.

Why grieve for the lost deer,
for the fish that clutter the brook,
the kingdoms of midge that cloud its surface,
the flocks of birds that come to feed.
The earth does not grieve.
It rushes toward the season of waste—

On the porch the weather shifts,
the cat dispatches
another expendable animal from the field.
Soon she will go inside to cull her litter,
addressing each with a diagnostic tongue.
Have I learned nothing? God,
into whose deep pocket our cries are swept,
it is you I look for
in the slate face of the water.

SWEET EVERLASTING

Swarming over the damp ground with pocket lenses
that discover and distort like an insect's
compound eye, the second grade
slows, stops at the barrier on the path.
They straddle the horizontal trunk, down for months;
rub the rough track of the saw, then focus
on the new shoots at the other end—
residual, suggestive.
I follow the children into open land
above the orchard, its small clouds tethered
to the grass, where we gather
samples of the plentiful white bud
that stipples the high pasture, and name it
by the book: wooly stem, pale lanceolate leaves;
the one called Everlasting. The punishment for doubt
is doubt—my father's death has taught me that.
Last week, he surfaced in a dream as promised,
as, at night, the logic of earth subsides
and stars appear to substantiate
what we could not see. But when I woke,
I remembered nothing that could tell me
which among those distant pulsing inconclusive signs
were active, which extinguished—
remembered, that is,
nothing that could save him.

from ❧

THE LOTUS FLOWERS

1987

Man is in love and loves what vanishes.

—W. B. YEATS

THE LAST CLASS

Put this in your notebooks:
All verse is occasional verse.
In March, trying to get home, distracted
and impatient at Gate 5 in the Greyhound station,
I saw a drunk man bothering a woman.
A poem depends on its detail
but the woman had her back to me,
and the man was just another drunk,
black in this case, familiar, dirty.
I moved past them both, got on the bus.

There is no further action to report.
The man is not a symbol. If what he said to her
touches us, we are touched by a narrative
we supply. What he said was, "I'm sorry,
I'm sorry," over and over, "I'm sorry,"
but you must understand he frightened the woman,
he meant to rob her of those few quiet
solitary moments sitting down,
waiting for the bus, before she headed home
and probably got supper for her family,
perhaps in a room in Framingham,
perhaps her child was sick.

My bus pulled out, made its usual turns
and parted the formal gardens from the Common,
both of them camouflaged by snow.
And as it threaded its way to open road,
leaving the city, leaving our sullen classroom,
I postponed my satchel of your poems
and wondered who I am to teach the young,
having come so far from honest love of the world;
I tried to recall how it felt
to live without grief; and then I wrote down
a few tentative lines about the drunk,
because of an old compulsion to record,
or sudden resolve not to be self-absorbed
and full of dread—
                                    I wanted to salvage
something from my life, to fix
some truth beyond all change, the way
photographers of war, miles from the front,
lift print after print into the light,
each one further cropped and amplified,
pruning whatever baffles or obscures,
until the small figures are restored
as young men sleeping.

VISITING THE GRAVES

All day we travel from bed to bed, our children
clutching homemade bouquets of tulips and jonquils,
hyacinth, handfuls of yellow salad from the fields.
In Pittsylvania County, our dead face east,
my great-grandfather and his sons facing
what is now a stranger's farm. And here
is my father, under the big oak, near the stone
we watched him weep beside for twenty years,
and my mother beside him, the greenest slab of grass.
By horse, it was hours to Franklin County,
to Liberty Christian Church where her mother lies—
the children squabble in the car, roll on the velvet
slope of the churchyard, pout or laugh as we point out
the gap in the mountain where *her* mother's grave
is underwater, the lake lapping the house, the house
still standing like a tooth. We tell them how
we picked huckleberries from the yard,
tell them what a huckleberry is, but the oldest
can't keep straight who's still alive, the smallest
wants her flowers back—who can blame them,
this far from home, tired of trying
to climb a tree of bones. They fall asleep
halfway down the road, and we fall silent too,
who were taught to remember and return,
my sister is driving, I'm in the back,
the sky before us a broken field of cloud.

THE PHOTOGRAPH

Black as a crow's wing was what they said
about my mother's hair. Even now,
back home, someone on the street
will stop me to recall my mother,
how beautiful she was,
first among her sisters.
In the photograph, her hair
is a spill of ink below the white beret,
a swell of dark water. And her eyes as dark,
her chin lifted, that brusque defining posture
she had just begun in her defense.
Seventeen, on her own,
still a shadow in my father's longing—nothing
the camera could record foretold
her restlessness, the years of shrill
unspecified despair, the clear reproach
of my life, just beginning.

The horseshoe hung in the neck of the tree sinks
deeper into heartwood every season.
Sometimes I hear the past
hum in my ear, its cruel perfected music,
as I turn from the stove
or stop to braid my daughter's thick black hair.

THE FIELD TRIP

This time they're thirteen, no longer
interested in the trillium on the path but in each other,
though they will not say so. Only the chaperone
lingers at the adder's-tongue,
watching the teacher trail the rest uphill
to where the dense virginal forest thins and opens.
At the clearing, she tells them to be still and mute
and make a list of what they see and hear.
A girl asks if she should also list
the way she feels—she's the one
who'll cite the shadow on the lake below.
The others sprawl on gender-separate rocks
except for the smart-ass, perched
on the cliff-edge, inviting front-page photos—
PICNIC MARRED BY TRAGEDY. From time to time,
in the midst of the day's continual lunch,
as the students read the lists their teacher edits,
the boy swears and stretches—
he is in fact fourteen, doing seventh grade
a second time, this same assignment
also a second time. Pressed, he says
he sees exactly what he saw before—ponds, rocks, trees—
shouting it back from the same vantage point
out on the twelve-inch ledge,
Long Pond a ragged puddle underneath him;
and what he shouts grows more and more

dangerously insubordinate as he leans
more and more dramatically over the edge.
But he is, after all, the first to spot the hawk;
and it is, looking down on it, amazing. The others
gather near the unimpeded view,
together, finally, standing on this bluff
overlooking three natural ponds, hearing the wind
ruffle the cedar fringe, watching the hawk
float along the thermals like a leaf.
And for a moment, belittled by indifferent wilderness,
you want to praise the boy, so much does he resemble
if not the hawk then the doomed shrub
fanned against the rockface there beside him,
rooted in a fissure in the rock.
But soon the hero swings back up to earth,
the group divides. Just like that
they're ready for home, tired of practicing:
sixteen children, two adults, and one
bad boy who carved a scorpion on his arm.

THE TRUST

Something was killing sheep
but it was sheep this dog attended on the farm—
a black-and-white border collie, patrolling his fold
like a parish priest. The second time the neighbor came,
claiming to have spotted the dog at night, a crouched figure
slithering toward the pen on the far side of the county,
the farmer let him witness how the dog,
alert and steady, mended the frayed
edge of the flock, the clumped sheep calm
as they drifted together along the stony hill.
But still more sheep across the glen were slaughtered,
and the man returned more confident. This time,
the master called his dog forward,
and stroking the eager head, prized open the mouth to find,
wound around the base of the back teeth—squat molars
the paws can't reach to clean—small coils of wool,
fine and stiff, like threads from his own jacket.
So he took down the rifle from the rack
and shot the dog and buried him,
his best companion in the field for seven years.
Once satisfied, the appetite is never dulled again.
Night after night, its sweet insistent promise
drives the animal under the rail fence and miles away
for a fresh kill; and with guilty cunning brings him back
to his familiar charges, just now stirring in the early light,
brings him home to his proud husbandry.

THE FARMER

In the still-blistering late afternoon,
like currying a horse the rake
circled the meadow, the cut grass ridging
behind it. This summer, if the weather held,
he'd risk a second harvest after years
of reinvesting, leaving fallow.
These fields were why he farmed—
he walked the fenceline like a man in love.
The animals were merely what he needed:
cattle and pigs; chickens for awhile; a drayhorse,
saddle horses he was paid to pasture—
an endless stupid round
of animals, one of them always hungry, sick, lost,
calving or farrowing, or waiting slaughter.

When the field began dissolving in the dusk,
he carried feed down to the knoll,
its clump of pines, gate, trough, lick, chute
and two gray hives; leaned into the Jersey's side
as the galvanized bucket filled with milk;
released the cow and turned to the bees.
He'd taken honey before without protection.
This time, they could smell something
in his sweat—fatigue? impatience,
although he was a stubborn, patient man?
Suddenly, like flame, they were swarming over him.

He rolled in the dirt, manure and stiff hoof-prints,
started back up the path, rolled in the fresh hay—
refused to run, which would have pumped
the venom through him faster—passed the oaks
at the yard's edge, rolled in the yard, reached
the kitchen, and when he tore off his clothes
crushed bees dropped from him like scabs.

For a week he lay in the darkened bedroom.
The doctor stopped by twice a day—
the hundred stings "enough to kill an ox,
enough to kill a younger man." What saved him
were the years of smaller doses—
like minor disappointments,
instructive poison, something he could use.

BRIGHT LEAF

Like words put to a song, the bunched tobacco leaves
are strung along a stick, the women
standing in the August heat for hours—since first light—
under the pitched tin roof, barefoot, and at their feet
the babies, bare-assed, dirty, eating dirt.
The older children hand the leaves from the slide,
three leaves at a time, stalks upright, three handers
for each stringer, and three more heaped canvas slides
waiting in what little shade there is: it's ten o'clock,
almost dinnertime. They pull the pails of cold lunch
and Mason jars of tea out of the spring
when they see the farmer coming from the field, their men
stripped to the waist, polished by sweat and tired as mules.
By afternoon, the loose cotton dresses, even
the headrags are dark with sweat.
Still their fingers never miss a stitch,
though they're paid not by the stick but by the day,
and the talk—unbroken news of cousins and acquaintances—
unwinding with the ball of twine, a frayed snuff-twig
bouncing on one lip, the string paying out
through their calluses, the piles of wide green leaves
diminishing, until the men appear with the last slide
and clamber up the rafters of the barn
to line the loaded sticks along the tiers. It's Friday:

the farmer pays with a wad of ones and fives,
having turned the mule out to its feed and water,
hung up the stiffened traces and the bit. He checks
again the other barns, already fired, crude ovens
of log and mud where the crop is cured;
in that hot dry acrid air, spreads a yellowing leaf
across his palm, rolls an edge in his fingers,
gauging by its texture and its smell
how high to drive the fire.
His crew is quiet in the pickup truck—did you think
they were singing? They are much too tired to even speak,
can barely lick salt from the back of a hand, brush at flies,
hush a baby with a sugartit. And the man
who owns this land is also tired.
Everyday this week he's meant to bring home pears
from the old tree by the barn, but now he sees
the fruit has fallen, sees the yellow jackets feeding there.
He lights a Lucky, frames a joke for his wife—he'll say
their banker raised a piss-poor field this year.
And she will lean against the doorjamb
while he talks, while he scrubs his hands at the tin basin
with a split lemon and a pumice stone, rubs them raw
trying to cut the gummy resin, that stubborn
black stain within the green.

AMARYLLIS

Having been a farmer's daughter
she didn't want to be a farmer's wife, didn't want
the smell of ripe manure in all his clothes,
the corresponding flies in her kitchen,
a pail of slop below the sink,
a crate of baby chicks beside the stove, piping
beneath their bare lightbulb, cows calling at the gate
for him to come, cows standing in the chute
as he crops their horns with his long sharp shears.
So she nagged him toward a job in town;
so she sprang from the table, weeping, when he swore;
so, after supper, she sulks over her mending
as he unfolds his pearl pocketknife
to trim a callus on his palm.
Too much like her mother, he says, not knowing
any other reason why she spoils the children,
or why he comes in from the combine with his wrenches
to find potatoes boiled dry in their pot,
his wife in the parlor on the bench
at her oak piano—not playing
you understand, just sitting like a fern
in that formal room.
                    So much time to think,
these long hours: like her mother,
each night she goes to bed when her husband's tired,
gets up when he gets up, and in between tries

not to move, listening to the sleep of this good man
who lies beside and over her. So much time alone,
since everything he knows is practical.
Just this morning, he plunged an icepick
into the bloated side of the cow unable to rise,
dying where it fell, its several stomachs having failed—
too full, he said, of sweet wet clover.

NIGHTSHADE

The dog lay under the house, having crawled
back beyond the porch, bellying
beneath the joists through rocks and red dirt
to the cool stone foundation where it died
as the children called and sobbed;
and now their father had to wrench it out,
the one he had been breaking to handle birds.

This was a man of strictest moderation,
who had heard a dash of strychnine in its meat
could be a tonic for a dog, an extra edge.
He loved that dog, and got the dosage wrong.
And I loved my father—
I was among the children looking on—
and for years would not forgive him:

without pure evil in the world,
there was no east or west, no polestar
and no ratifying dove. I sat inside
the small white house for hours,
deaf to the world, playing my two songs,
one in a major, the other in a sad, minor key.

THE WATERFALL

Meeting after twenty years apart,
I ask my friend to give me back myself
at nineteen, but he can't, or won't:
Sunny, he says, and quick to speak your mind.
Then he asks if he has aged,
if he looks the same—who had always seemed
so satisfied, past need, past harm.
At every stop we stare at each other,
returning to the other's face as though
it were a wind-rucked pond we hope will clear.
And slowly, as we spiral up the mountain,
looking for landmarks, the road
a narrow shelf on the wooded slopes, I realize
he's terrified of me; and since he cannot yet
know who I am, begin to see myself as I was then:
implacable:

              but that's not the word he flung at me
beside the shaded pool, the blanket smoothed,
the picnic barely opened. That was years ago;
now we have the usual pleasantries,
trade photographs, his family and mine,
their fixed improbable faces.

                      Eventually,
we find the general store, the left-turn fork,
the hidden waterfall still
battering the rocks,

and the ease of recognition makes me old.
Standing close enough to feel the spray,
looking up at the falls, its powerful
inexhaustible rush of water,
I think that art has ruined my life,
fraught as it is with what's exceptional.
But that's not true; at the start, at nineteen,
I wanted it all,
every exhilaration, every grief—

acquisitive was what he said.
How could I have hurt him?
Such a new candle, just lit, burning, burning.

DANCING WITH POETS

"The accident" is what he calls the time
he threw himself from a window four floors up,
breaking his back and both ankles so that walking
became the direst labor for this man
who takes my hand, invites me to the empty strip of floor
that fronts the instruments, a length of polished wood
the shape of a grave. *Unsuited for this world*:
his body bears the marks of it, his hand
is tense with effort and with shame, and I shy away
from any audience, but I love to dance—and soon
we find a way to move, drifting apart as each
effects a different ripple across the floor,
a plaid and a stripe to match the solid navy of the band.
And suddenly the band is getting better, so pleased
to have this pair of dancers, since we make evident
the music in the noise—and the dull pulse
leaps with unexpected riffs and turns, we can hear
how good the keyboard really is, the bright cresting
of another major key as others join us: a strict
block of a man, a formidable cliff of mind, dancing
as if melted, as if unhinged; his partner a gift of brave
elegance to those who watch her dance; and at her elbow
Berryman back from the bridge, and Frost, relieved
of grievances, Dickinson waltzing there with lavish Keats,
who coughs into a borrowed handkerchief—all the poets of exile
and despair, unfit for this life, all those who cannot speak

but only sing, all those who cannot walk
who strut and spin until the waiting citizens at the bar,
aloof, judgmental, begin to sway or drum their straws or hum,
leaving their seats to crowd the narrow floor
as though we were one body, sweating and foolish,
one body with its clear pathetic grace,
not lifted out of grief but dancing it, transforming
for one night this local bar, before we're turned back out
to our separate selves, to the dangerous streets and houses,
to the overwhelming drone of the living world.

FEAST DAY

If you wanted to hang a sprig of mistletoe,
you had to shoot it down from the tree. Summers,
with so much dense proliferation at the horizon,
the eye was caught by weed and bush, grapes
sprawling on a low fence, hedgerows of wild rose
or privet hedge, a snarl of honeysuckle, blackberry
along the red gash the road made, and kudzu overtaking
the banks, the rotting logs, a burnt-out barn.
But in winter, from a distance, scanning the hills,
you could easily spot a clump of mistletoe
in the high oak, the topmost branches—
like a nest against the gray sky,
and closer, the only green thing left in the black tree.
After Advent, having tied the wreath of running cedar
and whacked a blue-tipped cedar out of the field;
having unearthed the white potatoes and the yams
and brought the pears and peaches off their shelf;
having sweated all the sugar from the sorghum
and plucked the doves; having long since
slaughtered the hog and swung it by the heels in a nearby tree,
boiled and scraped the bristles, slabbed the ribs,
packed the hams in salt, rinsed and stuffed the gut,
plunged the knuckles into brine, having eaten the testicles
and ground the snout with any remaining parts to make a cheese,
you went upcountry with your gun.

                              O mild Christ,
now everyone is gathered. The parents
quarreling with their one remaining son,
sisters locked in cruel competition—the centerpiece
on the wide plank table is pyracantha, thorn of fire,
torn from a low shrub beside the house.
And lifted above us: emblem of peace, emblem of affection,
with its few pearls, its small inedible berry.

SHORT STORY

My grandfather killed a mule with a hammer,
or maybe with a plank, or a stick, maybe
it was a horse—the story varied
in the telling. If he was planting corn
when it happened, it was a mule, and he was plowing
the upper slope, west of the house, his overalls
stiff to the knees with red dirt, the lines
draped behind his neck.
He must have been glad to rest
when the mule first stopped mid-furrow;
looked back at where he'd come, then down
to the brush along the creek he meant to clear.
No doubt he noticed the hawk's great leisure
over the field, the crows lumped
in the biggest elm on the opposite hill.
After he'd wiped his hatbrim with his sleeve,
he called to the mule as he slapped the line
along its rump, clicked and whistled.

My grandfather was a slight, quiet man,
smaller than most women, smaller
than his wife. Had she been in the yard,
seen him heading toward the pump now,
she'd pump for him a dipper of cold water.
Walking back to the field, past the corncrib,
he took an ear of corn to start the mule,

but the mule was planted. He never cursed
or shouted, only whipped it, the mule
rippling its backside each time
the switch fell, and when that didn't work
whipped it low on its side, where it's tender,
then cross-hatched the welts he'd made already.
The mule went down on one knee,
and that was when he reached for the blown limb,
or walked to the pile of seasoning lumber; or else,
unhooked the plow and took his own time to the shed
to get the hammer.
                                By the time I was born,
he couldn't even lift a stick. He lived
another fifteen years in a chair,
but now he's dead, and so is his son,
who never meant to speak a word against him,
and whom I never asked what his father
was planting and in which field,
and whether it happened before he married,
before his children came in quick succession,
before his wife died of the last one.
And only a few of us are left
who ever heard that story.

STONE POND

Driving over the limit
on a mountain road,
the mist rising, Stone Pond
white with ice and white mist
inside its circle
of birch and black fir:

driving home after
seeing friends, the radio
complicitous and loud,
Beethoven's braided musical line,
a sonata I recall
playing well:

passing the tiny houses
on the hillside, woodsmoke
rising among the budded trees,
then passing within inches
of someone's yard:
I circle Stone Pond, and despair

seems like something I can set aside.
The road bends again, the morning
burns through the mist.
Sufficient joy—
what should I have done to make it last?

THE LOTUS FLOWERS

The surface of the pond was mostly green—
bright green algae reaching out from the banks,
then the mass of waterlilies, their broad round leaves
rim to rim, each white flower spreading
from the center of a green saucer.
We teased and argued, choosing the largest,
the sweetest bloom, but when the rowboat
lumbered through and rearranged them,
we found the plants were anchored, the separate
muscular stems descending in the dense water—
only the most determined put her hand
into that frog-slimed pond
to wrestle with a flower. Back and forth
we pumped across the water, in twos and threes,
full of brave adventure. On the marshy shore,
the others hollered for their turns,
or at the hem of where we pitched the tents
gathered firewood—
                            this was wilderness,
although the pond was less than half an acre
and we could still see the grand magnolias
in the village cemetery, their waxy
white conical blossoms gleaming in the foliage.
A dozen girls, the oldest only twelve, two sisters
with their long braids, my shy neighbor,
someone squealing without interruption:

all we didn't know about the world buoyed us,
as the frightful water sustained and moved the flowers
tethered at a depth we couldn't see.

In the late afternoon, before they'd folded
into candles on the dark water,
I went to fill the bucket at the spring.
Deep in the pines, exposed tree roots
formed a natural arch, a cave of black loam.
I raked off the skin of leaves and needles,
leaving a pool so clear and shallow
I could count the pebbles
on the studded floor. The sudden cold
splashing up from the bucket to my hands
made me want to plunge my hand in—
and I held it under, feeling the shock that wakes
and deadens, watching first my fingers,
then the ledge beyond me,
the snake submerged and motionless,
the head propped on its coils the way a girl
crosses her arms before her on the sill
and rests her chin there.
                              Lugging the bucket
back to the noisy clearing, I found nothing changed,
the boat still rocked across the pond,
the fire straggled and cracked as we fed it

branches and debris into the night,
leaning back on our pallets—
spokes in a wheel—learning the names of the many
constellations, learning how each fixed
cluster took its name:
not from the strongest light, but from the pattern
made by stars of lesser magnitude,
so like the smaller stars we rowed among.

from ❧

TWO TREES

1992

THE INNOCENTS

Not as one might slip into a stream,
though it is a stream,
nor as we slide from sleep or into sleep,
but as the breath of a passing animal
unmoors a spore from the lacy frond
is the soul brought out of heaven.

It is another buoyancy.
With only the briefest fitfulness
the mote hangs in the vapor above the pond,
the crumb rides at the end of the supple line
on the skin of the river
until the slick fish swallows.

    One fish, two fish, how many of God's fish
    swam out of the sea?

    Muskrat, mud rat, does the toothed water rat
    still hunt in the sea?

    Night bird, nested bird, who drew the whistling bird
    so far from the sea?

    Red fox, brown fox, can any hungry silver fox
    remember the sea?

AT THE PIANO

At the piano, the girl, as if rowing upstream,
is driving triplets against the duple meter,
one hand for repetition,
one hand for variation and for song.
She knows nothing, but Bach knows everything.
Outside, in the vast disordered world,
the calves have been taken from their mothers;
both groups bawled and hooted all night long—
she heard them from her quilted double bed.
Twice a day, she gives the young
their frothy warm placebo. While her brother
steadies the cow with grain, her sister
leans in close from the little stool,
fingertips aligned on the wrinkled tits
as if to pick some soft, fleshy fruit
but pressing in, hard, while pulling down,
she milks with both hands, two jets of milk
spraying the metal pail as they go in.
The girl must put her whole hand in the pail
and push the head of the suckling toward it:
wet muzzle, corrugated tongue.
Last year's calf is in the bank. On the mantel,
brass candlesticks, twinned again in the mirror,
and the loud squat clock, her metronome.
At the piano, hands in her lap—
what's given, and what's made from luck and will—

she also hears a diaphonic moan:
long before dusk the animals in the pens
again have started calling for each other,
either hungry or too full, she can't tell
which is which. Her mother's in the kitchen,
her father's in the hayloft pitching hay,
she pushes off in her wooden boat—
she knows nothing, she thinks
no one could be happier than this.

VARIATIONS: AT THE PIANO

The almost visible wall
is made of sound.
It keeps the girl apart
as she prefers,
as long as her fingers
press the even keys,
as long as the household
hears the web of sound
spun from the loom.

Outside, in mild
or terrible weather, trees
bud, flower, leaf out,
lose leaves. Inside,
the king and queen have swooned,
the castle swoons.

Wall of glass, of gauze.

True pitch:
when the eye can hear,
when the ear names what's heard:
the mind becomes a second instrument.

Transposing the world to one mathematic *A*,
she envies how the others
steer by the wake of any passing ship.
Fixed to a fixed star, she becomes the star—
that distant—
a flare in the crowded heavens.

The day is foul—a thin sleet falling everywhere,
the slops of it congealing on the street
with trash, soot, smog and general grime,
the sky's dark clouds incarnate underfoot,
buses, cars, people, rats, roaches
flooding the street with their effluvia.
Inside the studio, it's high summer,
eighteenth-century rational Germany.
On the open score a meadow blooms, the notes
flowers on their upright stems, the pianist
harvesting from each its grain of sound—
she has, that is, the undeflected focus
of a bee, and from the concert grand
the fugue emerging—

                        see how it seduces,
what carries no mark of the present world,
no news, no merchants, no murderous weather,
no crude alarms, no lives lost or saved.

This far inland, after the hurricane,
wind on the porch sufficient
to chuff and ravel the tangled "baby's-tears"
disturbs the cluster of chimes:
five separate oriental tones
in endless permutations—both pattern and not pattern—
as the central lozenge is stirred to strike
each of the five suspended metal rods,
the five sounds of the black piano keys.
It makes a lullaby—

                      she loves the sane
intervals of the chimes, although in a recent dream
she drove the grand piano down the road
and found no place to park it.
After a life of music the musician said,
"But music, music has nothing to do with life."

"Earthy, exuberant, full of gusto,
bristling with intelligence.

And the tips of your fingers were so very small."
He leans across her arm to pour the wine.

Since thirty years have passed he can admit
he envied her her gifts—

perhaps mistakes that envy for desire,
like David on the throne hearing the harp.

And now remembers the slope of her white neck;
and now is sure that neck's improved with age.

Digging a hole to where the past is buried,
one covers the living grass on either side.

AFTER KEATS

1.

If truth is not a thing apart from me,
then I don't want it.

2.

   —Have you always told the truth?

I have always loved the truth.

WOMAN WHO WEEPS

Up from the valley, ten children working the fields
and three in the ground, plus four who'd slipped like fish
from a faulty seine, she wept to the priest:
    Father, I saw the Virgin on a hill,

    she was a lion, lying on her side,

    grooming her blonde shoulders with her tongue.

Six months weeping as she hulled the corn,
gathered late fruit and milked the goats,
planted grain and watched the hillside blossom,
before she went to the bishop, kissed his ring.
    Father, I saw Our Lady in a tree,

    swaddled in black, she was a raven,

    on one leg, on one bent claw

    she hunched in the tree but she was the tree,

    charred trunk in a thicket of green.

After seven years of weeping,
not as other stunned old women weep,
she baked flat bread, washed the cooking stones,
cut a staff from a sapling by the road.
The Holy Father sat in a gilded chair:
    Father, I saw Christ's Mother in a stream,

    she was a rock, the water

    parted on either side of her,

    from one stream she made two—

two tresses loosened across her collarbone—
until the pouring water met at her breast
and made a single stream again.

Then from the marketplace, from the busiest stall
she stole five ripened figs
and carried her weeping back to the countryside,
with a cloth sack, with a beggar's cup,
village to village and into the smoky huts,
her soul a well, an eye, an open door.

TWO TREES

At first, for the man and woman,
everything was beautiful.
Which is to say there was no beauty,
since there was not its opposite, its absence.
Every tree was "pleasant to the sight,"
the cattle also, and every creeping thing.

But at the center, foreground of the painting,
God put two trees, different from the others.
One was shrubby, spreading near the ground
lithe branches, like a fountain,
studded with fruit and thorns.
When the woman saw
this tree was good for food
and a tree to be desired to make one wise,
she ate,
      and also saw
the other, even more to be desired,
tallest in the garden, its leaves
a deeper green than all the rest,
its boughs, shapely and proportionate,
hung with sweet fruit that never fell,
fruit that made the birds nesting there
graceful, brightly plumed and musical,
yet when they pecked it showed no scar.

To eat from both these trees was to be a god.
So God kept them from the second fruit,
and sent them into thistles and violent weather,
wearing the skins of lesser beasts—
let them garden dust and stony ground,
let them bear a child who was beautiful,
as they had been, and also bear a child
marked and hateful as they would become,
and bring these forth from the body's
stink and sorrow while the mind cried out
for that addictive tree it had tasted,
and for that other, crown still visible
over the wall.

VARIATIONS: TWO TREES

Pretty face, pretty girl,
what was the camouflage that afternoon—
the way you stooped to hide your breasts?
the scabs you'd wheedled into your upper arm?
The others left to tour the reptile house;
inside the tent of net
we stood as still as trees to watch the birds.
On the woodchip path, scratching like chickens,
a toucan and a smaller cockatoo
were magnets for the eye, vivid and thus exotic.
Then I heard it: on a low-slung branch
the dove so near we could have touched it, throat
puffed like a bellows between the tiny head and fat butt—

Every seditious thought I ever thought
is in her head; and in her mouth
its best expression—
                    murderous,
murderous thoughts of those we love:
what other hell is this seductive, the self
self-justified, stopping its ears?

And where in nature is the paradigm,
except the first division of the cell?
No compassion encoded there,

but one of us must speak with its voice,
as if the other were the animal
gnawing the caught paw free.

Sleek, blue, the jays are beautiful
until they speak. She used to say
that when they cry like that, a gargle

harsh as the rusted handle of a pump,
there'll soon be rain:
she could hear the liquid in their voices.

He can't remember much of what she said:
his ear is less retentive than his eye,
and when she spoke

he was busy watching her mouth
dimple and pout, her mouth
painted as he liked it.

These days he thinks of her infrequently—
when the jay calls, when the fox
shrieks in the field like a thing imperiled—

and yet with other women,
moths on a screen,
his eye will trigger something in his mind

like sound. *Siren* is the word
for what he hears, beauty's warning:
within its pleasures, all its urgencies.

Because it is a curse to be beautiful
and thus dismissed by other men,
the pretty man often wants to marry
mind, or grit, or great heart undistracted.
This is not the same as the lovely woman
who marries someone plain; she knows
the world's assessment has been wrong, knows
she is a fraud and proclaims it
with that mirror. The handsome man feels
no such scorn: yes, he is as gorgeous
as they say, but it's not a useful currency,
except with the plain woman who marries him
as one would pocket found-money or plant a rose.
But the plain man, the homely man, the man
hunched like a cricket or built like a jug,
who marries beauty and covets his own wife,
the man who prays at the altar of his wife,
the man who weeps when he has her, weeps when she's gone—
remember Menelaus, how he burned?

When the deaf child came to school they tied his hands.
They meant to teach him speech, the common language.
They meant to cast him down into silence
      only a little while.
They showed him their teeth, their pink gymnastic tongues.
And raised him up with exaggerated praise
      if his face made the shapes their faces made,
      if he made his mouth a funnel for the sound
            and opened his throat to let the angel out.

His hands lay on his desk as though they were sick.
Like the two sick chimps he saw at the zoo.
One ran to the wire—knuckles swept the ground—
      rolling her lips under, exposing the gums.
The other was turned away from his audience,
      fingers and opposable thumbs
            stripping the leaves from a wand of the tree.
Perhaps it would be a tool; perhaps, a weapon.

Slender, cylindrical,
without a mark or seam,
almost wet against the rock;
wearing alternating bands
of black and yellow, and itself
coiled like a bracelet.

           "Pretty, pretty,"
is what the baby said, reaching for it.

SOFT CLOUD PASSING

I.

Ice goes out of the pond as it came in—
from the edges toward the center:

large translucent pupil of an eye.

If the dream is a wish,
what does she wish for?

Soft cloud passing between us and the sun.

2.

The plucked fields,
the bushes, spent and brittle,
the brown thatch on the forest floor
swoon beneath the gathered layers of gauze
before the earth is dragged once more into blossom.

And the woman at the window, watching the snow,
news of the child just now upon her—
she has the enviable rigor of the selfish,
light that seems so strong because withheld.
Already she cannot recall her former life.
She puts her face against the glass
as though listening.

Deer yarded up in the bog,
dogpack looking for deer.

3.

The child is hot to her hand, less on his white
forehead beneath the damp foliage of hair
than in the crevices of thigh, belly, knee, dumpling-foot.
The telephone on the desk is a lump of coal.
She fans him with a magazine, she sponges
his limbs, her hands move up and down
as if ironing: this is how she prays,
without a sound, without closing her eyes.
When daylight was first sufficient to see the snow
falling, fine as sugar, it seemed an answer,
God chilling the world to save a child,
although she knows that isn't how it works.
Her husband naps in a chair;
doctor three blocks over, drugstore on the corner—
how often she walked past, pushing the stroller.
She lifts the baby closer to her heart.
The streets are clear, the sky clear, the sun
radiant and climbing:
the shelf of her breast will have to be the snow.
And so she holds him tighter, tighter,
believes she feels him cooling in her arms.

EFFORT AT SPEECH

Nothing was as we'd thought, the sea
anemones not plants but animals,
flounder languishing on the sand
like infants waiting to be turned—
from the bottom we followed the spiral ramp
around and up, circling the tank.
Robert, barely out of the crib,
rode his father's shoulders, uttering
words or parts of words and pointing
ceaselessly toward the water, toward
one of the many shapes in the water,
what he could not name, could not describe.
Starfish, monkfish—not fish—catfish,
sea hare, sea horse: we studied the plaques
for something to prompt him with,
but he tucked his head as if shamed.
So I left them at the school of the quick
yellow-with-black-stripes conventional,
passed the armored centenary
turtle going down as I went up,
seaweed, eels, elongate gun-gray suede
bodies of the prehistoric sharks
traversing the reef, and headed to the top,
thinking to look down through the multiple layers.
When it first came at me, it seemed more
creature of the air than of the sea,

huge, delta-winged, bat-winged,
head subsumed in the spread pectorals—
unless it was all head—a kite
gliding to the wall between us, veering
up, over, exposing its light belly,
"face" made by gill-slits opening,
the tail's long whip and poison spine.
Eagle Ray: *cordata*, like the eagle;
it skated along the glass—
eagle scanning the sheer canyon wall,
bat trapped inside the cave,
no, like a mind at work, at play,
I felt I was seeing through the skull—
and then away.

SONG AND STORY

The girl strapped in the bare mechanical crib
does not open her eyes, does not cry out.
The glottal tube is taped into her face;
bereft of sound, she seems so far away.
But a box on the stucco wall, wired to her chest,
televises the flutter of her heart—
news from the pit—her pulse rapid and shallow,
a rising line, except when her mother sings,
outside the bars: whenever her mother sings
the line steadies into a row of waves,
song of the sea, song of the scythe

       old woman by the well, picking up stones
       old woman by the well, picking up stones

When Orpheus, beating rhythm with a spear
against the deck of the armed ship, sang
to steady the oars, he borrowed an old measure:
broadax striking oak, oak singing back,
the churn, the pump, the shuttle sweeping the warp
like the waves against the shore they were pulling toward.
The men at the oars saw only the next man's back.
They were living a story—the story of desire,
the rising line of ships at war or trade.
If the sky's dark fabric was pierced by stars,
they didn't see them; if dolphins leapt from the water,

they didn't see them. Sweat beaded their backs
like heavy dew. But whether they came to triumph
or defeat, music ferried them out
and brought them back, taking the dead and wounded
back to the wave-licked, smooth initial shore,
song of the locust, song of the broom

      old woman in the field, binding wheat
      old woman by the fire, grinding corn

When Orpheus, braiding rushes by the stream,
devised a song for the overlords of hell
to break the hearts they didn't know they had,
he drew one from the olive grove—
the raven's hinged wings from tree to tree,
whole flocks of geese crossing the ruffled sky,
the sun's repeated arc, moon in its wake:
this wasn't the music of pain. Pain has no music,
pain is a story: it starts,
Eurydice was taken from the fields.
She did not sing—you cannot sing in hell—
but in that viscous dark she heard the song
flung like a rope into the crater of hell,
song of the sickle, song of the hive

old woman by the cradle, stringing beads

old woman by the cradle, stringing beads

The one who can sing sings to the one who can't,
who waits in the pit, like Procne among the slaves,
as the gods decide how all such stories end,
the story woven into the marriage gown,
or scratched with a stick in the dust around the well,
or written in blood in the box on the stucco wall—
look at the wall:
the song, rising and falling, sings in the heartbeat,
sings in the seasons, sings in the daily round—
even at night, deep in the murmuring wood—
listen—one bird, full-throated, calls to another,
little sister, frantic little sparrow under the eaves.

from

KYRIE

1995

Nothing else—no infection, no war, no famine—
has ever killed so many in as short a period.

—ALFRED W. CROSBY,
America's Forgotten Pandemic: The Influenza of 1918

All ears, nose, tongue and gut,
dogs know if something's wrong,
chickens don't know a thing, their brains
are little more than optic nerve—
they think it's been a very short day
and settle in the pines, good night,
head under wing, near their cousins
but welded to a lower branch.

Dogs, all kinds of dogs—signals
are their job, they cock their heads,
their backs bristle, even house dogs
wake up and circle the wool rug.
Outside, the vacant yard: then,
within minutes something eats the sun.

Dear Mattie, You're sweet to write me every day.
The train was not so bad, I found a seat,
watched the landscape flatten until dark,
ate the lunch you packed, your good chess pie.
I've made a friend, a Carolina man
who looks like Emmett Cocke, same big grin,
square teeth. Curses hard but he can shoot.
Sergeant calls him Pug I don't know why.
It's hot here but we're not here for long.
Most all we do is march and shine our boots.
In the drills they keep us twenty feet apart
on account of sickness in the camp.
In case you think to send more pie, send two.
I'll try to bring you back some French perfume.

When does a childhood end? Mothers
sew a piece of money inside a sock,
fathers unfold the map of the world, and boys
go off to war—that's an end, whether
they come back wrapped in the flag or waving it.
Sister and I were what they kissed goodbye,
complicitous in the long dream left behind.
On one page, willful innocence,

$\qquad\qquad\qquad\qquad\qquad$ on the next

an army captain writing from the ward
with few details and much regret—a kindness
she wouldn't forgive, and wouldn't be reconciled
to her soldier lost, or me in my luck, or the petals
strewn on the grass, or the boys still on the playground
routing evil with their little sticks.

To be brought from the bright schoolyard into the house:
to stand by her bed like an animal stunned in the pen:
against the grid of the quilt, her hand seems
stitched to the cuff of its sleeve—although he wants
most urgently the hand to stroke his head,
although he thinks he could kneel down
that it would need to travel only inches
to brush like a breath his flushed cheek,
he doesn't stir: all his resolve,
all his resources go to watching her,
her mouth, her hair a pillow of blackened ferns—
he means to match her stillness bone for bone.
Nearby he hears the younger children cry,
and his aunts, like careless thieves, out in the kitchen.

This is the double bed where she'd been born,
bed of her mother's marriage and decline,
bed her sisters also ripened in,
bed that drew her husband to her side,
bed of her one child lost and five delivered,
bed indifferent to the many bodies,
bed around which all of them were gathered,
watery shapes in the shadows of the room,
and the bed frail abroad the violent ocean,
the frightened beasts so clumsy and pathetic,
heaving their wet breath against her neck,
she threw off the pile of quilts—white face like a moon—
and then entered straightway into heaven.

When it was time to move, he didn't move,
he lay athwart his mother. She pushed and pushed—
she'd had a stone before, she wanted a child.

Reaching in, I turned him like a calf.
Rob gave her a piece of kindling wood,
she bit right through. I turned him twice.

Her sisters were all in the house, her brother
home again on leave—

                       in the months to come
in the cities there would be families
reported their terminals and fled,

                                volunteers
would have to hunt the dying door-to-door.

It started here with too many breech and stillborn,
women who looked fifty not thirty-two.
I marked it childbed fever in my log.

Dear Mattie, Pug says even a year of camp
would not help most of us so why not now.
Tomorrow we take a train to New York City,
board a freighter there. You know how the logs
are flushed through the long flume at Hodnetts' Mill,
the stream flooding the sluice, the cut pines
crowding and pushing and rushing, and then
the narrow chute opens onto the pond?
I'll feel like that, once we're out to sea
and seeing the world. I need to say
I've saved a bit, and you should also have
my grandpa's watch—tell Fan that I said so.
Keep busy, pray for me, go on with Life,
and put your mind to a wedding in the yard.

In my sister's dream about the war
the animals had clearly human expressions
of grief and dread, maybe they were people
wearing animal bodies, cows at the fence,
hens in their nests. The older dog implored her
at the door; out back, aeroplanes
crossing overhead, she found the young one
motionless on the grass, open-eyed,
left leg bitten off, the meat and muscles
stripped back neatly from the jagged bone.
For weeks I thought that was my fiancé,
the mailbox was a shrine, I bargained with
the little god inside—I didn't know
it was us she saw in the bloody trenches.

My father's cousin Rawley in the Service,
we got word, and I think a neighbor's infant,
that was common, my mother'd lost one too.

Then he went to town to join the war.
The sheriff hauled him home in an open rig:
spat on the street, been jailed a week or two.

She ran from the henhouse shrieking, shaking eggs
from the purse of her white apron to the ground.

Before I was born, he built a wide oak drainboard
in the kitchen, didn't just glue the boards,
screwed them down. Glue held, one split in two.

My mother was an angel out of heaven.
My father was a viper. I wished him dead,
then he was dead. But she was too.

My brothers had it, my sister, parceled out
among the relatives, I had it exiled
in the attic room. Each afternoon
Grandfather came to the top stair, said
"How's my chickadee," and left me sweet
cream still in the crank. I couldn't eat it
but I hugged the sweaty bucket, I put
the chilled metal paddle against my tongue,
I swam in the quarry, into a nest of ropes,
they wrapped my chest, they kissed the soles of my feet
but not with kisses. Another time: a man
stooped in the open door with her packed valise,
my mother smoothing on eight-button gloves,
handing me a tooth, a sprig of rue—

O God, Thou hast cast us off, Thou hast scattered us,
    Thou hast been displeased, O turn to us again.
Thou hast made the earth to tremble; Thou hast broken it;
    heal the breaches thereof; for it shaketh.
Thou hast showed Thy people hard things; Thou hast made us
    to drink the wine of astonishment.

Surely He shall deliver us from the snare,
He shall cover us with His feathers, and under His wings,
    We shall not be afraid for the arrow by day
    nor for the pestilence that walketh in darkness.
A thousand shall fall at our side, ten thousand shall fall,
    but it shall not come nigh us, no evil befall us,
Because He hath set His love upon us. . . .

                      Here endeth the first lesson.

All day, one room: me, and the cherubim
with their wet kisses. Without quarantines,
who knew what was happening at home—
was someone put to bed, had someone died?
The paper said how dangerous, they coughed
and snuffed in their double desks, facing me—
they sneezed and spit on books we passed around
and on the boots I tied, retied, barely
out of school myself, Price at the front—
they smeared their lunch, they had no handkerchiefs,
no fresh water to wash my hands—when the youngest
started to cry, flushed and scared,
I just couldn't touch her, I let her cry.
Their teacher, and I let them cry.

Dear Mattie, Did you have the garden turned?
This morning early while I took my watch
I heard a wood sparrow—the song's the same
no matter what they call them over here—
remembered too when we were marching in,
the cottonwoods and sycamores and popples,
how fine they struck me coming from the ship
after so much empty flat gray sky,
on deck winds plowing up tremendous waves
and down below half the battalion ill.
Thirty-four we left behind in the sea
and more fell in the road, it's what took Pug.
But there's enough of us still and brave enough
to finish this quickly off and hurry home.

You wiped a fever-brow, you burned the cloth.
You scrubbed a sickroom floor, you burned the mop.
What wouldn't burn you boiled like applesauce
out beside the shed in the copper pot.
Apple, lightwood, linen, feather bed—
it was the smell of that time, that neighborhood.
All night the pyre smouldered in the yard.
Your job: to obliterate what had been soiled.

But the bitten heart no longer cares for risk.
The orthodox still passed from lip to lip
the blessed relic and the ritual cup.
To see in the pile the delicate pillowslip
she'd worked by hand, roses and bluets—
as if hope could be fed by giving up—

A large lake, a little island in it.
Winter comes to the island and the ice
forms along the shore—when the first got sick
others came in to nurse them and it spread,
ice reaching out from the island into the lake.
Of course, there was another, larger shore—
Germany and Spain, New York, Atlanta,
ice also building *toward* the island.
By ice I'm thinking just those in the ground;
the sickness was more like brushfire in a clearing,
everyone beating the brush with coats and hands,
meanwhile the forest around us up in flames.
What was it like? I was small, I was sick,
I can't remember much—go study the graves.

The barber, the teacher, the plumber, the preacher,
the man in a bowler, man in a cap,
the banker, the baker, the cabinet-maker,
the fireman, postman, clerk in the shop,

soldier and sailor, teamster and tailor,
man shoveling snow or sweeping his step,
carpenter, cobbler, liar, lawyer,
laid them down and never got up.

O, O, the world wouldn't stop—
the neighborhood grocer, the neighborhood cop
laid them down and never did rise.
And some of their children, and some of their wives,
fell into bed and never got up,
fell into bed and never got up.

How we survived: we locked the doors
and let nobody in. Each night we sang.
Ate only bread in a bowl of buttermilk.
Boiled the drinking water from the well,
clipped our hair to the scalp, slept in steam.
Rubbed our chests with camphor, backs
with mustard, legs and thighs with fatback
and buried the rind. Since we had no lambs
I cut the cat's throat, Xed the door
and put the carcass out to draw the flies.
I raised an upstairs window and watched them go—
swollen, shiny, black, green-backed, green-eyed—
fleeing the house, taking the sickness with them.

Oh yes I used to pray. I prayed for the baby,
I prayed for my mortal soul as it contracted,
I prayed a gun would happen into my hand.
I prayed the way our nearest neighbors prayed,
head down, hands wrung, knees on the hard floor.
They all were sick and prayed to the Merciful Father
to send an angel, and my Henry came.
The least of these my brethren, Henry said.
Wherefore by my fruits, Henry said.
All of them survived—and do you think
they're still praying, thank you Lord for Henry?
She was so tiny, we kept her in a shoebox
on the cookstove, like a kitten.

Sweet are the songs of bitterness and blame,
against the stranger spitting on the street,
the neighbor's shared contaminated meal,
the rusted nail, the doctor come too late.

Sweet are the songs of envy and despair,
which count the healthy strangers that we meet
and mark the neighbors' illness mild and brief,
the birds that go on nesting, the brilliant air.

Sweet are the songs of wry exacted praise,
scraped from the grave, shaped in the torn throat
and sung at the helpful stranger on the train,
and at the neighbors misery brought near,
and at the waters parted at our feet,
and to the god who thought to keep us here.

I cried unto God with my voice . . . he gave ear unto me.
In the day of my trouble I sought the Lord;
 my sore ran in the night, and ceased not;
 my soul refused to be comforted.
 I remembered God, and was troubled;
 I complained, and my spirit was overwhelmed.
I am so troubled I cannot speak.

Will the Lord cast off for ever? Is his mercy
 clean gone for ever? does his promise fail
 for evermore? Has God forgot to be gracious?
 has he in anger shut up his tender mercies?

Who is so great a God as our God?
 who has declared his strength among the people.

Who said the worst was past, who knew
such a thing? Someone writing history,
someone looking down on us
from the clouds. Down here, snow and wind:
cold blew through the clapboards,
our spring was frozen in the frozen ground.
Like the beasts in their holes,
no one stirred—if not sick
exhausted or afraid. In the village,
the doctor's own wife died in the night
of the nineteenth, 1919.
But it was true: at the window,
every afternoon, toward the horizon,
a little more light before the darkness fell.

Dear Mat, For the red scarf I'm much obliged.
At first I couldn't wear it—bright colors
draw fire—but now I can. We took a shell
where three of us were washing out our socks
in a crater near my post. Good thing
the sock was off my foot since the foot's
all to pieces now—don't you fret,
it could have been my head, I've seen that here,
and then what use would be your pretty scarf?
The nurse bundles me up like an old man,
or a boy, and wheels me off the ward,
so many sick. But the Enemy suffers worse,
thanks to our gawdam guns as Pug would say.
Victory will come soon but without me.

The bride is in the parlor, dear confection.
Down on his knee at the edge of all that white,
her father puts a penny in her shoe.

Under the stiff organza and the sash,
the first cell of her first child slips
into the chamber with a little click.

The family next door was never struck
but we lost three—was that God's will? And which
were chosen for its purpose, us or them?

The Gospel says there is no us and them.
Science says there is no moral lesson.
The photo album says, who are these people?

After the paw withdraws, the world
hums again, making its golden honey.

No longer just a stream, not yet a pond,
the water slowed and deepened, banks eroded,
redwing blackbird roosting on a stalk,
sometimes that rippled vee plowing the surface.
Each clear day, she walked to the willow oak,
raked the anemic grass, tidied the mounds,
walked back down to the house by way of the creek.
If the beaver had put in a stick, she took it out.
If a storm had dropped a branch, she hauled it off.
When milder weather came, she tucked her skirts
at the waist and waded in, dislodging trash
the beaver would recover. Months of this.
Twice she sent for the neighbor to trap it or shoot it,
but each time Fan said Emmett don't you dare.

Once the world had had its fill of war,
in a secret wood, as the countryside lay stunned,
at the hour of the wolf and the vole, in a railroad car,
the generals met and put their weapons down.
Like spring it was, as word passed over all
the pocked and riven ground, and underground;
now the nations sat in a gilded hall,
dividing what they'd keep of what they'd won.

And so the armies could be done with war,
and soldiers trickled home to study peace.
But the old gardens grew a tough new weed,
and the old lives didn't fit as they had before,
and where there'd been the dream, a stranger's face,
and where there'd been the war, an empty sleeve.

Around the house uneasy stillness falls.
The dog stiffens the ruff at her ears,
stands, looks to the backdoor, looks to the stairwell,
licks her master's shoe. What she hears

must be a pitch high on the Orphic scale,
a light disturbance in the air,
like flicks of an insect's wings or a reed's whistle
distant and brief: he barely stirs.

Out in the kitchen something seems to settle—
cloth on a dish, dust on a chair?
The animal whimpers now but doesn't growl:
this absence has a smell.
                            Poor master,
it's touched him too, that shift in molecules,
but all he feels is more of what's not there.

My mother died, I was eight, I was sent away—
that has no meaning, just a shape,
the room I've lived in. That morning, end of May,

there'd been a frost so hard it looked like snow,
white on the green fields, the startled cows.
Spring in the fields, wild onion spikes the clover—

so bitter, even the butter ruined.
I've known some to dump it at the barn,
but if I bought a lamp that didn't burn

I wouldn't dump the oil, I'd soak the wick.
Eating a slice raw will do the work:
you notice nothing in the milk but milk.

To have inherited a child, angry
and grieving, to have opened her rusted heart
that first full inch; to feel it seize on the cold air
rushing in; and now to pretend his story,
lost in the deep thicket of the others,
is not hers: he stole again from the store,
she whipped him home and locked him in the barn,
he set the barn on fire and ran away.
How could that be her sister's boy, asleep
in the trundle bed, or ratcheting through the field—
he loved to be outside—from the porch she'd see
the top of his head, golden as the wheat,
parting the wheat, and then the wheat
closing up behind him without a seam.

What I remember best is my cousin's crow.
He found it, fed it, splinted its damaged wing,
and it came when he whistled it down, ate from his hand,
said, like a slow child, what he had said.
Emmett never used a leash or cage;
for a year it hulked in the big pine by the door
or in the windmill's metal scaffold, descending
for apple, a little grain, a little show.

Once God gave out free will, I bet He was sorry.
So much had been invested in the bird,
the bird not understanding gratitude.
Well again, it turned up in the yard
from time to time, no longer smart or amusing,
no longer *his*, just another crow.

Dear Mattie, Wanting this right I'll write it down.
At the rally, I signed up for the War.
My father wanted that, and Fan was there
with Del and Kate and A. T. Cocke, Rob
and Renie and their children waving flags,
the Hodnetts and the Foxes next to them,
Dr. Gilmore Reynolds on his porch,
and Rawley a hero in his uniform.
Your uncle held the Bible for the oath,
everyone cheered—could you and your sister hear it
down at the school? It was the best birthday,
are you proud of me, we hadn't thought
to be married anyway before the fall,
I should be home to bring the harvest in

Why did you have to go back, go back
to that awful time, upstream, scavenging
the human wreckage, what happened or what we did
or failed to do? Why drag us back to the ditch?
Have you no regard for oblivion?

History is organic, a great tree,
along the starched corduroy of its bark
the healed scars, the seasonal losses
so asymmetrical, so common—
why should you set out to count?

Don't you people have sufficient woe?

After the first year, weeds and scrub;
after five, juniper and birch,
alders filling in among the briars;
ten more years, maples rise and thicken;
forty years, the birches crowded out,
a new world swarms on the floor of the hardwood forest.
And who can tell us where there was an orchard,
where a swing, where the smokehouse stood.

from 〰

SHADOW OF HEAVEN

2002

. . . though what if Earth
Be but the shadow of Heaven, and things therein
Each to other like, more than on Earth is thought?

—*Paradise Lost*

LARGESSE

Aix-en-Provence

Banging the blue shutters—night-rain;
and a deep gash opened in the yard.
By noon, the usual unstinting sun
but also wind, the olive trees gone silver,
inside out, and the slender cypresses,
like women in fringed shawls, hugging themselves,
and over the rosemary hedge the pocked fig
giving its purple scrota to the ground.

What was it had made me sad? At the market,
stall after noisy stall, melons, olives,
more fresh herbs than I could name, tomatoes
still stitched to the cut vine, the soft
transparent squid shelved on ice; also,
hanging there beside the garlic braids,
meek as the sausages: plucked fowl with feet.

Under a goose-wing, I had a violent dream.
I was carrying a baby and was blind,
or blinded on and off, the ledge I walked
blanking out long minutes at a time.
He'd flung a confident arm around my neck.
A spidery crack traversed his china skull.
Then it was not a ledge but a bridge, like a tongue.

From the window over my desk, I could look down
at the rain-ruined nest the *sangliers*
had scrabbled in the thyme, or up, to the bald
mountain in all the paintings. I looked up.
That's where one looks in the grip of a dream.

WINTER FIELD

The winter field is not
the field of summer lost in snow: it is
another thing, a different thing.

"We shouted, we shook you," you tell me,
but there was no sound, no face, no fear, only
oblivion—why shouldn't it be so?

After they'd pierced a vein and fished me up,
after they'd reeled me back they packed me under
blanket on top of blanket, I trembled so.

The summer field, sun-fed, mutable,
has its many tasks; the winter field
becomes its adjective.
                        For those hours
I was some other thing, and my body,
which you have long loved well,
did not love you.

LONG MARRIAGE

Forward his numb foot, back
her foot, his chin on her head,
her head on his collarbone,

during those marathons
between wars, our vivid
Dark Times, each dancer holds

the other up so he,
as the vertical heap barely
moves yet moves, or she,

eyes half-lidded, unmoored,
can rest. Why these, surviving
a decimated field?

More than a lucky fit—
not planks planed from the same
oak trunk but mortise and tenon—

it is the yoke that makes
the pair, that binds them to
their blind resolve, two kids

who thought the world was burning
itself out, and bet
on a matched disregard

for the safe and the sad—*Look*,
one hisses toward the flared
familiar ear, *we've come*

this far, this far, this far.

LESSON

Whenever my mother, who taught
small children forty years,
asked a question, she
already knew the answer.
"Would you like to" meant
you would. "Shall we" was
another, and "Don't you think."
As in, "Don't you think
it's time you cut your hair."

So when, in the bare room,
in the strict bed, she said
"You want to see?" her hands
were busy at her neckline,
untying the robe, not looking
down at it, stitches
bristling where the breast
had been, but straight at me.

I did what I always did:
not weep—she never wept—
and made my face a freshly
white-washed wall: let her
write, again, whatever
she wanted there.

HIMALAYA

Branches: wings: we sheltered in thick fir trees.
The cliff-face, as we'd asked, had furnished trees.

When your mother died, I dreamed the wild mountain
of the grave, its myrrh and milk, fur and fleece.

I know what my soul saw: the sky like silk
pulled through a ring, a flock of wind-slurred trees.

Those feathery evergreens were blue—didn't you
wear blue for luck at all her surgeries?

Calm came into the dream, unburdened as snow.
It sugared the rocks, the rock-encircled trees.

You had no need to dream her back: your many
kisses were locks against death's burglaries.

Regret came into the dream thankless as snow.
It floured God's black beard, it furred the trees.

There was no pile of stones, laid one by one
to mark the leaden anniversaries.

No beasts, no birds—snow fine as smoke, and the only
quickened shapes, behind that curtain, were trees.

Years past, a soul slipped by the stone I was.
On the windowpane, frost's rucked embroideries.

Root and branch: the year of fasting ends.
Outside: veiled sun, snow's layered silks, blurred trees.

Whose ghost is it, Shahid, feeds my grief-dream?
Whose loss, whose task, whose darkened nursery?

HIGH WINDS FLARE UP AND
THE OLD HOUSE SHUDDERS

The dead should just shut up. Already
they've ruined the new-plowed field:
it looks like a grave. Adjacent pine-woods,
another set of walls: in that dark room
a birch, too young to have a waist,
practices sway and bend, slope and give.
And the bee at vertical rest on the outside pane,
belly facing in, one jointed limb crooked
to its mouth, the mouth at work—
my lost friend, of course, who lifelong
chewed his cuticles to the quick. Likewise
Jane who calls from her closet of walnut and silk
for her widower to stroke her breasts, her feet,
although she has no breasts, she has no feet,
exacting pity in their big white bed.
The dead themselves are pitiless—
they keen and thrash, or they lodge
in your throat like a stone, or they descend
as spring snow, as late light, as light-struck dust
rises and descends—frantic for more, more of this earth,
more of its flesh, more death, oh yes, and a few more
thousand last vast blue cloud-blemished skies.

THE GARDEN, SPRING, THE HAWK

from Baton Rouge, to my sister in Virginia

I.

Like a struck match: redbird, riding the wet
knuckle of the longest limb of the leafless water oak,
pitching glissandi over the myrtle trees.
The yellow cat, one paw leveraged out of the soggy grass, then another,
has nothing to do with this: too slow, too old.
Nor the night-stunned snakes under the log, a cluster of commas;
nor the cloistered vole, the wasp, the translucent lizard,
the spider's swaddle of gauze, waiting to quicken.
This hour belongs to the birds—where I am,
single ripe berry on the bush; where you are,
Cooper's hawk, on the rail fence, dressing her feathers;
and the indistinct domestics at their chores.

2.

While the prodigal husband is still asleep,
and the half-grown child, also sleeping, breathes in and out
as if that were the dullest task—while the migraine
loosens its fist and the pulse slows, one
overeager chamber of the heart and one reluctant
pumping together, lifting the blood and its boats
across the locks,
                is it possible yet to sit
at the broad window, hands around a cup,
the furnace in a modest hum, and make your mind
the streaked, sweaty pane a rag rubs clear?
Tree: fence: frogpond the size of a tire: residual moon:
each a weight to hold the skull-flap down.

3.

The very air voluptuous and droll,
sometimes wrung into mist or vertical rain, Tuesday
breezes of shifting magnitudes, diaphanous cloud,
by Wednesday afternoon unsullied sun
but not hot—the season at this latitude
seems coy,
          seems feminine, I nearly said,
a woman napping in a frothy gown, and credit
thinking it
          not to having been away so long,
or the multitude of songbirds, courting and throbbing,
or the slutty blossoming of shrubs, but coming back
at all:
       the country of one's origin
is always *she*, the ground beneath the plow,

4.

and the Deep South a clearer paradigm
than where you live beside the northern gate:
or Carolina where I went to school among magnolias,
back row, far left, one more blank white face:

or the first hill at the junction of woods and field,
functional garden, random flowers unsolicited,
and beyond the redbrick house, houses we built
below the pines in the soft trash of the forest floor—
days, weeks, we colonized a wilderness; it needed that *we*,

and closed to both of us when you were twelve, thirteen.
Time to be groomed for the breathless hunt-and-run,
purse and title at the finish line.

5.

As if I were the moss, D. said, electric
and dismayed. House behind us scaffolded and draped
for surgery, she was showing me those hanks of woeful hair
harvested from live oaks down the street and rehung here;
it lives on air, like the gray Confederate ghosts
she sleeps among. Long-married, transplant, more guest
than host, she has a forced-resilience look (like my friend C.,
divorced last year, her heart prised like a root
from its tight pocket).
                              Scissors and trowel: saw and chisel:
D. hired someone to help her stay, to knock away a wall
and put in glass. Like yours: window over the table,
row of doors to bring the outside in.

6.

A back paw lifts: *adagio*: unlike
Thursday's cat harassing squirrels, untiringly,
that sallied forth from a clipped hibiscus, motoring
into open lawn where the hungry and the anxious
gathered food—hurry, hurry, they saw it coming on,
then leapt to a tree. After a long pause, the peril
hustled a straight line back to wait by the hedge.
Up and down the tree the squirrels flickered.
One by one they hazarded the ground.
Like criminals they angled toward the bread, nonchalant—
but spastic, too, their rigid compact bodies
ratcheting toward the source, the tree, the cat.

7.

Soft, sweet, fetching, idle, pliable—whose
ideal was that? And how should it fit a childhood
reaching under a chicken for an egg? Or grown sisters, come
with gardens on their heads, who, at the sink, uncorseted,
let loose high-pitched complaint and low burlesque
as they itemized the Women's Fellowship, assaying
pew by pew the match that each had made.

Took me years to like that company. Meanwhile,
little pitcher with brains, I could see the men
leaning against the Packard in the yard, smoking,
toeing the hard red dirt, analyzing crops and cash,
or politics and war, or—or what? The world.

8.

The slim successive cars like vertebrae
trailing the primitive skull, the train pulls forward,
past other trains and disconnected engines, Janus-faced;
negotiates the network of spurs and switches,
a thicket of poles and wires, sheer brick canyons,
signal-flags of laundry; passes the cotton mill's windows'
blind blue grid, and picks up speed downhill

as the late-model coupe turns left at the edge of town.
Windows open. Maps unpleated across the dash.
Something loud, popular and brisk, on the radio.

Now solve for x: how long, midday, they'll travel
neck and neck beside the broadening river. . . .

9.

Against the brown field, bare trees, the hawk
swivels her head: becomes a bird. Cousin to eagle and kite,
marked like the smaller male she mates for life,
all that's vivid kept to the underside,

she doesn't touch the bread, the scraps of meat
you leave for the crows—it's mistakes she's after,
reckless mole, fledgling in the grass. The kitten
stays inside, hare in its hole. And you:
you've also learned to be good at holding still.

Why does a thing so fierce need camouflage?
Cooper's hawk, chicken hawk—you've seen her fly:
short wing-beats, and then the long glide.

10.

Like an unsheathed falcon to the falconer
you *flew*, at eighteen, to his outstretched arm.
Restricted, addictive plural:

                      and with it, your one
vocation. Why so eager for received idea?
This was not an absence of ambition but the heart thrown
like a rubbed coin. . . .

                   Harder now to wish, harder to choose,
something in you drained off, or worn away,
and not yet, in its place, a new resolve—

you said so, late last fall, under the dead
limbs of the largest dogwood in the yard:
I can't even imagine a different life.

And spaded in another dozen bulbs.

II.

My beautiful capable daughter, far from home
where rocks outnumber blossoms, had this dream:

I'd planted the steep hillside behind the house,
mostly vegetables, and they were huge: my secret
was salt, in which the bell peppers thrived and fruited,
and lush tomatoes, flowers on the barn's south side,
the path down through them littered with purple roses
(only the clenched, introverted heads), I'd put them there,
purple her favorite so I knew she'd follow
the bend in the brook to the level field which was—
I'd planted this too—a broad expanse of white lace,
web of froth and steel: wedding gown.

12.

Again and again the low-slung campus cat
charged out and back entirely purposeful.
that is, mechanical: in fact, remote-controlled
by a pleasant, detached young man behind the hedge,
studying Caution versus Appetite.
Clipboard, stopwatch, food, known patch of grass—
for the foragers, a closed set: he was measuring
how near his subjects let the danger come
before they bolted for the tree. Although by then
I could see it wasn't a very plausible cat,
remnants of shag glued to a model car,
it was hard to feel superior to the squirrels.

13.

The cardinal sings and sings: hunter's horn;
then, artillery. The round red door to its heart
is always open. And now the same song
from down the street, this time a mockingbird,
which, like the emperor's toy, can do it better.

How many generations did it take to cultivate, in us,
the marriage gene? Or, if we simply learned our lessons well,
didn't you see it, smell it, in that air:
to loathe change is to loathe life—

                              Nevermind.
What you want from me is only an ear. Meanwhile,
the carpenter has come in his rusted truck
(Echo also does this bird quite well).

14.

Once, there was a king with two daughters.
The older girl of course would take the throne.
And so it was left to the other to be clever.

Lead lute for the Young and Foolish Virgins,
she rode her great blue ox across the moat;
having a thorn in its hoof, it *needed* a friend.

She underwent the seven grueling labors.
She wrote a symphony. She wrote checks home.
Next, a sweet boy's rescue from the tower.

She cut his hair, he baked her bread, and soon
they were lumbering magnolias coast to coast—
it's that spilt seed strewn out across the heavens.

15.

In the grass a beetle takes a quarter-turn;
in a week a window where there'd been a wall.
My hosts, plural and solicitous, apologize for winter's
monochrome, despite the fluent azalea, hibiscus, camellia—
whole trees of that soft fabric—aggressive bird:
one hundred shades of red. And basting the yard's edge
like stitches for a hem, like string at the mouth of a purse,
like a threading pulse, the cat prowls half-blind
among the shrubs. The student, asked if he had named
his cat, answered fast and earnest: "Oh no.
This is science." Intending, perhaps, like the exile,
to keep a little distance from what we are.

THE ART OF DISTANCE

I.

Wrinkle coming toward me in the grass—no,
fatter than that, rickrack, or the scallops a ruffle makes,
down to about the fourteenth vertebra. The rest of it: rod
instead of a coil.
                   So I'd been wrong the afternoon before
when the dog, curious, eager to play and bored with me
as I harvested the edge of the raspberry thicket,
stalked it from the back stoop to the lip
of the bank and grabbed the tip
in her mouth and tossed it—
sudden vertical shudder
shoulder-level—
                   wrong
to read survival in its cursive
spiraling back to the cellar window-well
where it had gathered field mice like a cat.
And now, if it meant to be heading for the brook,
it veered off-course, its blunt head raised
like a swimmer's in distress.
                   The functioning part
gave out just short of me, inside the shade
but not the bush; the damaged part,
two fingers thick, was torqued
pale belly up, sunstruck.

I left it where it was,
took the dog in, and for hours
watched, from the kitchen window, what seemed
a peeled stick, the supple upper body that had dragged it
now pointed away and occluded by the shade,
the uncut grass.
                    My strict father
would have been appalled: not to dispatch
a uselessly suffering thing made me the same, he'd say,
as the man who, seeing a toad,
catatonic Buddha in its niche, wedged
within the vise of a snake's efficient mouth
clamped open for, then closing slowly down and over it,
bludgeoned them both with the flat side of a hoe.

For once I will accept my father's judgment.
But this had been my yard, my snake, old enemy
resident at the back side of the house. For hours,
the pent dog panting and begging, I watched
from the window, as from a tower wall,
until it vanished: reluctant arrow
aimed at where the berries
ripened and fell.

2.

My father was an earth-sign and a stoic,
an eldest child, a steward, who took dominion
over the given world—at least, it seemed,
his hundred acres of it, pets we ate,
rabbits minced in the combine, inchling moths
torched in the crotch of the tree to save the peaches.
Scorned excess and complaint. Importuned,
said *no, not, can't, never will.*

                    What didn't fit
was seeing him cry. He'd stand alone in the field
like a rogue pine that had escaped the scythe,
as he would stand beside the family graves,
a short important distance from the car
where we were hushed until the white flag
had been unpocketed, and he jangled his keys
and got back in, not ever looking at us,

not looking at the brisk instructive face
my mother used on clerks, on amputees.
This all happened long before my mother,
in charge of cheerfulness and world morale,
had lost a body-part and given up—
so it was never in response to her,
the way he wept, or equally the way

he moved through life, one hoof after another:
a sentimental man is singular,
still the boy whose mother's gone away.
The last full day of our last ritual visit—
he'd taken a turn already into the field—
what set him off was hearing the neighbor's gun.
She merely wanted the turtle out of her beans;

he hauled the carcass home, two feet wide,
a rock from the creek, and also elderly
if the shell's whorls correspond to xylem and phloem,
rings we'd count on the cut trunk of a tree.
"Tastes like chicken," he said, gathering
the saw, the maul, chisel, pliers, hatchet
he'd need to unhouse the body and chop it up.

No one wanted to help, or even watch,
except the child intent on the row of knives,
and the child changing her mind with a webbed foot's wave—
dinner was not quite dead—but shudders and tears
were weakness and wouldn't work, jokes wouldn't work
on temper alchemized from noun into verb
as my father pried the armored plates apart,

pale and sweating and silent. And never did he,
sun long gone down, once quit the bloody porch,
the bowl of the upper shell in shards, the entrails
bejeweled with flies, the beaked head, feet and tail
cast off into wet grass, until, at the screen,
holding a platter of meat, he might have been
the Queen's woodsman bringing back the heart.

I heated the oil until it spit at me,
dredged the pieces in flour as I would chicken,
flung them chunk by chunk into the pan.
When chewed undefeated lumps ringed even his dish,
he said I'd done the best I knew, not
naming the skill: deflecting sorrow and terror
into a steady fierceness, and aiming *that*.

3.

They shaved the torso from behind the nape, across the shoulder
        to the center chest, taking away exactly the noble ruff
            and adjacent sable winter-thickened fur,

        making, when she crouches at my feet, the joint and sinew
            discernible under the startled skin,
                as in those close-up photos from the Veldt,
                as if she were hunched above a slack gazelle

        (but when she's sleeping on her side, her neck, extended,
            might be the slack gazelle's).

Fifty-seven stitches track from the spine,
        inside the sheltering ridge of the collarbone,
            down to where the trachea enters lung,
        their puckered, punctuated seam gathering
            what something split apart, some creature
                cornered in the woods or field,

no trophy, no raw meat except her own, no carcass
        pinioned now beneath her paws,
                            only the wretched quilt,
        torn and stained—

an obedient, courteous dog, she is abashed to pee indoors,
　　she doesn't squat, she stands with her head low,
　　　　like a whipped horse, as the gush puddles the floor—

and even though (or because) mostly when I touch her it is
　　to apply the many therapies prescribed, pills
　　　　down her throat, hot compress on the draining wound,
　　or to smooth the pallet of her lying-in,

she neither whimpers loudly nor draws back:

therefore, she seems not only dutiful
　　but grateful, too, as though the touch conveyed
　　　　a recognition; a bond
　　　　　　if not of pain, indignity;
　　　　compassion not for another but for oneself.

　　Which makes my hand enact a tenderness.
Like the rough warm tongue that licks the weak one clean.

4.

When you saw your father last, he was tied into a chair
with a soft sash: the nurses had parked him, nearly
weightless, near the window, in sunlight: the shook
filaments of fine white hair repelled

every bead of light as his tremorous head drooped on its stalk—
the whole stalk drooped, curving down and in, the chin
sank toward the concave chest, the arms were veined
sticks from the sleeves of the gown like a sack,

but his hands, delicate, unlined, *deliberate*, were reaching
forward as a small child might reach to stroke the warm
bright beam that struck his knees.
                                        "Still a doc,"
the charge-nurse said behind you at the door,

"still wants to diagnose." Said: the knees sometimes show
how close death is. A puffiness? Or granulated skin?
You didn't ask, seeing the focused will he lived by,
the avid mind, take its scientific measure,

the tips of the fingers glossing both kneecaps, comparing
each to each? Or, to the many patients in his head?
The rest of the body barely moved, except its slow
declension, the labored breaths so slow

and far apart: as though to practice for the long deep dive
the great sea-creatures make, only matched in humans
by the held moments when its brain shuts down
in order that the infant be delivered.

5.

After lunch, on the side porch,
the uncinched wooden leg in a muddy boot
stood by the edge of the bed. Freed from the second boot:
a full-length human leg, denim on white chenille. The other
stopped at a blunt substantial thigh. Its puckered stump,
facing me, looked like a face, or a fist.
I looked at it hard.

Four hands, three legs and half
a brain, my uncle said: what my grandmother
salvaged from the war—her brother's wounded sons,
sullen Ed with his limp, Grover hunched and simpering.
They worked the fields and in the barn, ate in her kitchen,
hair slick from washing up, like the hired hands.
When she said grace,

my grandmother said it standing,
bandaging her hand in her apron skirt
to lift the cast-iron skillet out of its round hole
to the square table of men. Burn herself up, her daughters said,
on Sundays, visiting like me, and scolding my uncle,
but still she fed with her fingers the squat stove,
and her grown wards

chopped the wood and hauled it,
pumped water, hauled it, cut hay, hauled it, hauled
the pig and cow and chicken shit and stirred the flies.
You keep out of the barn, my uncle said, after he'd found me
rapt by what they'd found: thick braid hung from a beam—
two blacksnakes writhing there like a hot wire,
a lit fuse.

What else do you need to know?
That my uncle, who was the baby, who went to war
and came home whole, who had no children, had no brothers,
thereby got the farm, would sell the farm—my uncle brought home,
for Grover, a puppy that liked to sleep in my grandmother's lap
and lick her plate, dirty little dog
her daughters said;

and a slick red racing bike,
which was not, with its manual brakes, the joke you think:
Ed stretched his crutch on the rack of the handlebars, slued
the stiff leg out and pumped the other, his sly pleasure breaking
through perfected scorn, cruising the porch where I sat
hulling peas in a china bowl—sometimes
the world looks back.

6.

The enormous world shimmering—
    then, in the magic glass, some of it,
        guessed at, came clear.

Whereas my friend "in nature"
    takes his glasses off so he
        "can think." When he says

he thinks with his body—body
    grown substantial over the years,
        as has his thought—

I don't know what he means; or,
    if I do, I think thinking is not
        the body's job,

that the body gets in the way.
    Our friendship feeds on argument.
        Each of us

has one prominent eye:
    his the one on the right, for the left
        side of the brain,

language and logic; but mine—
  wide and unforgiving—mine
   is the one on the left,

enlarged by superstition
  and music, like my father's more
   myopic eye.

Detachment is my friend's
  discovery, what he commends
   against despair.

And though my father claimed
  I never listen, of course I do:
   after all, who else

but the blind will lead the blind?
  And the years bring their own correction:
   to see a thing

one has to push it away.

7.

What art, like money, does is dig things up,
so that each tree and bush has its plateau—
tufts of frond in palms five stories high;
the spare flamboyant tree that seeds in pods,
its bunched florets; frangipani trees
to sweeten the air, clusters of white blossoms
with yellow throats; the mangrove trees, from whose
dense canopies descend the branch-like roots,
serpentine; and close to the ground, hedges
of bougainvillea, odorless, origami,
sometimes two colors on a single branch—
all rescued from the wet interior,
its undivided green, its bamboo swamps,
its breadfruit, mango, cocoa, guava, plum,
its forests of nutmeg trees, of almond trees—

Nobody needs be hungry here, excepting
what they wants is meat, Carlton said
when you remarked an isolated goat,
skeletal, among papaya trees.
Carlton's Tours are in his Chevrolet
(tan '68 sedan, original clutch),
and Carlton, wearing a tie, means to please,
courtly, bluffing when he doesn't know,

although he knows the flora, and where to find
abandoned factories that once made rum,
and overgrown plantations, and also where
the aborigines last took their stand:
on a bare cliff, so that, having lost again,
they could, and did, fling themselves to the sea.

One needs, it seems, sufficient irony:
to see oneself and the island as from the clouds:
a speck on the back of a gecko turning brown
these weeks before the rains, as if to hide
from the gray square-headed bird, its needle-nose,
its white chest and belly and underwing
blazed blue as it skims the azure swimming pool.
Past some small blackbirds, and the doctor-bird,
black with a blue face, who works like a bee
the oleander bush; past the cheery
banana-quit, across powdery sand,
raked everyday; and past broad-leaved sea grapes,
squat trees outposted near a ruffling surf:

How are you today? she says, and you say
Thank you, fine, and how are you? and she says
Not as fine as you, and she is right:

you could buy a room in the new hotel,
and she cannot afford the ferry off.
Want my pretty? she says, proffering
her grass baskets, loofahs still in their shells,
and bowls made from the gourds of a calabash tree,
which also serve—she models one—as hats.
Don't want to burn, she says, and even though
your skin has never been so white, so soft,
you tell her Not today, and look at the sea:

past riffling waves, past gulls cresting the tide
like boats, past sun-struck sails, a pencil line
divides dove gray and blue from navy blue,
partitioning the heavens from the earth.
And every day at dusk, released from under
the mangrove's raised umbrella, that cupped hand
overturned and pouring out, bats come
to reattach us—not with the tiny stitches
trawlers make against the far horizon,
but like a loom's ratcheting shuttle, weaving
first a net, then a veil, and then a shroud.

HORACE: ODE I.xxxiv

Parcus deorum cultor . . .

Lazy in praising or praying to any god
and madly rational, a clever captain
cruising the open seas of human thought,

now I must bring my vessel full about,
tack into port and sail back out again
on the route from which I strayed. For the God of gods,

who slices through the storm with flashes of fire,
this time in a clear sky came thundering
with his storied horses and his chariot,

whereby the dumb dull earth and its fluttering streams—
and the River Styx, and the dreaded mouth of the cave
at the end of the world—were shaken. So the god

does have sufficient power after all
to turn the tables on both high and low,
the mighty humbled and the meek raised up—

with a swift hiss of her wings, Fortune swoops down,
pleased to place the crown on this one's head,
as she was pleased to snatch it away from that one.

AUTUMN IN THE YARD WE PLANTED

Whoever said that I should count on mind?
Think it through, think it up—now that I know so much,
what's left to think is the unthinkable.

And the will has grown too tired to stamp its foot.
It sings a vapid song, it dithers and mopes,
it takes its basket to the marketplace,
like a schoolgirl in her best dress, and watches
others ask outright for what they want—
how do they know what they want?—and haul it away,
the sweet, the dull, the useless and the dear.

A maudlin, whimpering song: in which I lament
my own children, scything their separate paths
into the field, one with steady strokes, one
in a rage. We taught them that. And,
not to look back: at the apple tree, first
to shatter its petals onto the clipped grass,
or the slovenly heads of the russet peonies,

or even that late-to-arrive pastel, all stalk
with a few staggered blossoms, meadow rue—
though surely they could see it from where they are.

PRACTICE

To weep unbidden, to wake
at night in order to weep, to wait
for the whisker on the face of the clock
to twitch again, moving
the dumb day forward—

is this merely practice?
Some believe in heaven,
some in rest. *We'll float,*
you said. *Afterward*
we'll float between two worlds—

five bronze beetles
stacked like spoons in one
peony blossom, drugged by lust:
if I came back as a bird
I'd remember that—

until everyone we love
is safe is what you said.

MESSENGER

new poems

2006

THE FEEDER

I.

Bright blossom on the shrub's green lapel—
within hours after we hang the feeder
beside the wild viburnum, a goldfinch lights there.

And then, next day, a rose-breasted grosbeak
posing for us, making us proud as though
we'd painted ourselves the bloody bib
on its puffed white chest: our first failing.

                                      Our second:
disappointment with the chickadees—
common and local—despite the sleek black cap,
clean white cheeks, acrobatic body.

But weren't the early gifts a promise?
We've hung fat meat from a nearby branch, wanting
large, crested, rare, rapturous,
redbird fixed on the bush like a ripe fruit.

2.

Whenever the grosbeak comes, he comes
with his harem, lumps plain as sparrows,

and doesn't merely eat but preens,
never to be mistaken for some other.

The goldfinch likes to travel in flocks—
several indelible males, jostling,

careening up to the feeder, then away,
each a child on a stick, galloping;

and females, less spectacular,
shades of green and brown mixed into the yellow,

better to subside into the foliage.

3.

It struts on the grass, like a crow but smaller,
or, the grackle, whose green head shines,
or the starling, aiming its golden eye,

or the "red-winged" with its gaudy flags,
but this bird, this bird crosses the grass
white stripe tucked, orange locked up.

Blackbird, blackbird, fly away.
Take sorrow with you when you go.
Raven, starling, grackle, crow.

Tricolored Blackbird, my favorite, my signature:
nobody knows for sure what it is
till it flies away.

4.

O poor little bird, little dull peewee
with your condescending name

is it enough merely to sing
with such a transparent song?

5.

Some: thistle; some: sunflower, cracked, already shelled.
But it's grease that wooed these out of the woods,
a pair, Hairy not Downy, we know this
from their size and not their call.

Why are they squeaking? Bigger
than the rest, not bullied by jays, seizing the stash,
swinging on it, drilling into it, one at a time
as the other clings to the trunk of the nearest pine
and waits its turn,
                    even the one with the red
slash on his head.

6.

Today: one wild turkey, more a meal than a bird,

refusing to stay with the others out in the field
bobbing for apples—
                    bobbing *up*, from a crouch
on the crusted snowpack, olympic leaps.
                                    They also fly,
improbable and brutally efficient, low to the ground;

and the tree they roost in
trembles.

7.

Late March: glazed over, here,
don't go near Virginia—

that stab of forsythia, cherry weeping,
redbud smeared on the hill,

and perched in my sister's dogwood,
seven elegant cardinals, each

wearing a crown like something
it had earned, and trumpeting.

8.

Suddenly there suddenly gone.
                                    Do they count
if they come not to the back yard but the front,
not to the feeder but the crabapple tree,
its ornaments dulled
by winter?
                Multiple, tufted,
pulled forward by the blunt beak
like dancers propelled by the head:
                                            cedar waxwings:
I almost missed them, looking the other way.

9.

Nothing at the feeder. Nothing at the bush.
It takes awhile before I see the shadow.

10.

So: she's found me here:
chief bird of my childhood,
gray, pillow-breasted,
only needed asking—
no, only the crumbs
of others' invitations.
She waddles beneath the feeder,
retrieving what she can
from the hulls, the debris dropped
to the grass by the glamorous birds,
thrusting her undersized head
forward and back, forward
and back again. And her call,
alto, cello, *tremolo*,
makes the life I've made
melt away.

DEATHBED

He woke from fitful sleep, his father said,
calling for his mother—why wasn't she there,
why would she leave him in darkness and in pain?

"And I had to tell him, as if for the first time—
it was for him again the first time—
his mother had long been dead. For me, that loss

had become a shard worn smooth inside my pocket.
For him, it was sharp, new, not possible.
He wailed like a baby, my poor bewildered child,

and could not be consoled, like a child."

THE HIVE

To do something with it: to make something of it:
language races alongside, any given minute,

anything that happens—flies ahead of it
or lags behind, looking for meaning, beyond us yet,

on which we feed. So when the child provides the perfect
utterance, at once profound and innocent, resident

mystic, parent thinks, *got to write that down*. Next step:
dinner party, rude guest, appalled wife of guest,

the spilled red wine, congealed meat, the spoils left
to be distilled by the host *on whom nothing is lost.*

And what if the wife or even the self-afflicted guest
is you? Or, if your friend/wife/mother has been beset:

you drive to Intensive Care and take along a book:
worse, you take your pencils—two, in case one breaks—

and little bits of paper handy in your pocket,
are you not a monster? But is the human mind not

monstrous in its secret appetites, its habits?
In the Common Room, room soured by hope, late at night,

intending kind distraction, you hear your own mouth asking
the father of Frank, who is dying, "what do you do for a *living*,"

the unforgivable word a marker for the thought:
however will he/would I survive? Monstrous to set

that thought aside. But on your barely legible scraps:
the phrases, the very words, preserved like bees trapped

in amber, in anger, in grief, in all that overwhelmed.
Again, again, again, frail wings beat as they hover

over the untranslated world, to find what we need
(*thicket blooming south of here*) and bring what they find

back to the humming, hungry, constricted hive.

HARVESTING THE COWS

Stringy, skittery, thistle-burred, rib-etched,
　　they're like a pack of wolves lacking a sheep
　　　　but also lacking the speed, the teeth, the wits—

they're heifers culled from the herd, not worth the cost
　　of feeding and breeding and milking, let loose on a hill
　　　　one-third rock, one-third blackberry bramble.

And now, the scrub stung black by hard frost,
　　here come the young farmer and his father,
　　　　one earnest, one wizened, wind-whipped, sun-whipped,

who make at the gate, from strewn boards and boughs,
　　a pen, and park at its near end the compact
　　　　silver trailer, designed for two horses—

it waits at the mouth of the rutted tractor-trail
　　descending through trees, an artificial gulley.
　　　　Up goes Junior, hooting, driving them down.

So much bigger than wolves, these sixteen cows:
　　head to flank or flank to scrawny flank,
　　　　they can't turn around; but what they know is *no*:

some splash over the walls of the small corral,
    one, wall-eyed, giddy, smashes away
        the warped plank that's propped on the far side,

crashing across alders and wet windfall
    in a plausible though explosive dance, which prompts
        another to aim herself at the same hole,

too late: the plank's back up, she's turned to the clump
    and soon swimming among them, their white necks
        extended like the necks of hissing geese,

but so much bigger than geese. When the younger man
    wraps one neck in his arms, the cow rears up
        and he goes down, plaid wool in shit-slicked mud;

so then the elder takes her by the nose—
    I mean, he puts two fingers and a thumb
        inside the nostrils, pulls her into the trailer.

The rest shy and bunch away from the gate;
    a tail lifts for a stream of piss; one beast
        mounts another—panic that looks erotic—

and the herdsmen try guile, a pail of grain
    kept low, which keeps the head of the lead cow low
        as though resigned, ready for the gallows.

The silver loaf opens, swallows them in,
    two by two by two, and takes them away.
        Hams need to be smoked, turkeys to be dressed out

here in Arcadia, where a fine cold spit
    needles the air, and the birch and beech let go
        at last their last tattered golden rags.

RUBATO

I.

For the action: hammers of walnut—*nussbaum*, "nut tree";
the pinblock, hard-grained beech;

the keyframe, oak; the keybed, pine;
the knuckles, rosewood. In the belly, to ripen the tone,

maple, mahogany, and ironwood,
also called "hornbeam." The soundboard

spruce, best ratio of strength to weight, once split
not sawed, strip after narrow strip,

one-ply like the back of a cello, pressed together,
over which the struck strings quiver.

2.

Two years after her only brother died,
Papa, prosperous, took her to Berlin
to the factory, pianos fresh from the forest.
Inside: sound of the burr and chisel.

In her sailor dress and straight blunt-cut black hair,
she tried the one too bright, the one too dark,
choosing *this* one, head bent over the keyboard,
lost inside her *Kinderszenen*

as the clerks, gathered to listen, drew up the papers,
and Papa, patting his weskit, smiling again,
shipped it home by train to Wagenfeld.
Lodged inside: first love, first power.

Then shipped it back to Berlin in '29:
she'd stamped her teenaged foot for the *avant garde*,
to be let loose in Berlin *unter den linden*.
Locked inside: her mother's weeping.

Then shipped it ahead of her to America,
with linens, crystal, silver, fine bone china,
what I married into, crates of Rhein wine.
Inside: "Rhapsody in Blue"—

3.

not what my parents might have played
if my father had ever learned how to play
and if my mother had ever played

anything other than her one song,
"The Moon Shines Tonight on Pretty Red Wing,"
which may have been the very song

she played the evening they first met,
playing it over the years on the prized upright
bought "on time," egg-money spent

on their three children, what they chose
when it still seemed the future could be chosen,
the world waiting for what they'd choose.

4.

Deep in Robert Schumann's Piano Concerto,
at the cadenza's end, the violins
at rest, bows lowered into their laps, and the Maestro
cradling his baton, the two French horns
shaking their spit out onto the floor, the oboe
keeping his reed moist in his mouth—when the grand
returns, after the solo *appassionato*,
triplets now set against the bold left hand,

when they pull themselves again to full attention,
ready to reinstate the common measure,
they first must listen and wait, wait and listen,
all forward movement stalled, while the piano
lists wheresoever she will: tempo rubato:
time taken from one note, given to another.

5.

More like the Amazon flute than the silver flute,
a layered sound and not a brilliant sound,

the Bechstein's rim being "radiant" not "reflective,"
not continuous but joined, the joint
where the box housing the action meets the curve.

Before it was ours we made for it a second
radiant chamber, one wall spruce, one pine,
scraping past the pastel cabbage roses,

the sheep-on-a-hill, the girl behind her hat
as in my parents' bedroom, the painted plaster.
Then sanded down the grain and oiled it back,

once a day for a week, once a week
for a month, each month for a year, year after year.

6.

Also for the action: to settle the hammers
and speed each note's decay: tiny leather
tethers, and nestled nearby, to absorb and cushion,
glued inside: felts made of wool,

as from the mill in Wagenfeld, known
for durable blankets. Or felts that were made of hair,
pallets of hair—think of what might sleep
inside Grandmother's Chesterfield,

or think of the shorn heads turned into ash,
Papa and Mama smuggled out through Spain,
the mill seized, *das Juden* scrawled on the wall;
inside: the songs of Mendelssohn.

And her first language bitter on her tongue,
her marriage growing decadent, remote,
her hands growing slowly stiff and gnarled;
inside: Brahms' last Capriccio;

and the wine waiting under the cellar stairs,
and three sons born and all of them insufficient,
and Wagenfeld long gone with its cupolas;
inside: Schumann's "Träumerei";

and Papa gone, and Mama mute from a stroke,
and the corks rotted, the wine now vinegar,
the Bechstein's action sludge, its soundboard cracked,
inside: Beethoven's "Pathétique."

7.

How many times the same imperative:
coming with younger brothers home from school,
finding the note, propped on the shut piano,
that must have seemed when she wrote it rational,
and then the siren, the deep chagrin, life
taken up again—
                       no wonder you hate "drama,"
any passionate speech "hysterical"
or worse: deliberate, someone's "agenda."

So the past is not a scar but a wound:
I've seen it breaking open.

8.

Every day since 1931,
the year your parents met under the lindens,

the year my parents met in someone's kitchen,
our neighbor born next door has written down

the weather in our little town, the weddings,
the births and deaths—it is, whatever the season,

the daily song she sings, and we are in it, our daughter, our son,
his daughter. Today, that child turns one

so I play Grieg, her countryman,
then play Schumann's "Kinderszenen,"

and then: ragtime, American stride left hand
a steady measurement, the free right hand

a stitch ahead of the beat, then a stitch behind,
the stammered math of feeling

while the chords, in their circle of fifths, shift down,
and you come down the stairs in your pajamas, listening—

it's a new song when someone listens—
as when my father brought me Sunday's hymn,

and we sat together at the cheap upright, on the narrow bench,
side by side like two birds on a branch

facing into the wind, and I played for him
note by hammered note the baritone.

REDBUD

Everywhere, like grass: toadflax, yellow coils
        a girl's pincurls. Overhead,
the purely ornamental fruits, whites and pinks

thick on the bough. And straight ahead, along the path,
        spice viburnum, exotic shrub
named for the smell its clustered flowers held—nutmeg—

that made St. Louis tropical. We walked a lush,
        vast, groomed preserve—*preserve* in the sense
meant by self-indulgent kings, and in the sense

meant by science: every bloom and bine and bole,
        each independent green was labeled,
that was what we loved. And at the center, bronzed:

Linnaeus, master of design, whose art it was
        to shepherd any living thing
into its proper pasture. There, foamflower. There,

lungwort, vernacular "Spilled Milk," leaf splashed with white,
        a graceful *pulmonaria*
in the language of greatest clarity which classifies

lilies and roses, rows of lilac. And here, at our feet,
      shade-drunk dark herb: wormwood, our word
for bitterness: an *Artemisia*, The Hunter,

goddess made incarnate on the ground, in whose name
      the avid mortal watching her
was torn apart. Where was *his* name? Where was his flower?

A cloud paused in the spring sky, and there came to us then,
      on the path, another blossoming.
Radiant in mauve, head to toe, back braced

as though to balance the weight of full breasts, one hand,
      gloved, lifted unthinking to pet
the back of the hair, the hair itself a lacquered helmet.

And what should we make of her height, her heft, the size of the feet,
      the gruff swagger in the gait:
we stared outright—it seemed all right to stare, like

Linnaeus, who'd ranked the stones, and sorted the plants by how
      they propagate and colonized
whatever crawls and swims and flies and bears live young?

Light by which I've lived, the wish to name, to know,
 the work of it, the cost of it—
if only I could be, or want to be, more like

that boy: ignorant, stunned, human.
 "Acteon," you said,
 by his own hounds torn asunder. And so
the brief shadow flickered and dissolved: the world

was ours again, the world like *this*, made less confused.
 And we strolled like kings back down the path,
past a redbud tree in plush white bloom.

THE TATTERED DRESS

The day the royal court came through our village—
many drums and flutes, grandfather monkeys
with faces like fists and jewels the size of fists,
each elephant its own tree of blossoms,
a tiger on a leash, a pair of peacocks—

the old emperor did not choose me:
he chose my delicate sister. Our poor family
shrieked and clapped and pulled their hair, thinking,
plenty rice each year. And what does *she* think,
in the emperor's lap, inside the palace walls?

I did not put away the beautiful clothes
but wear them out among the buffalo,
wear them out in the field, in the standing water,
the filthy water that breeds our meat and drink,
my bent back a flash of scarlet and gold

that scatters the ducks and aggravates the swine.
Why not? Do I have some other calling?
The dull human oxen point at me:
one-almost-chosen: what
the lesser gods thought I could withstand.

Their judgment too I can withstand.

PRAYER

Artemis—virginal goddess of the hunt, thus
    goddess of childbirth, protector of children, to whom
        agonized women can cry out—

was not a name I thought of, a place to send
    those sharp gasps, when you descended sideways,
        still swimming against the narrow walls of me;

or later, after, the low moans, the mews,
    as I throbbed like something flung from a great height
        and could not be appeased; or in between,

a keening, you by then presenting, the cord—
    the lifeline, tether, leash—lashed like a noose
        round and round your neck by so much swimming.

I think what I said, if saying is what I did,
    was *Sweet Jesus*, another virgin who knew
        the body is first and last an animal,

it eats, shits, fucks, expels the fetus—or doesn't.
    Midnight, lamplight in the barn, the farmer,
        arm deep in the cow, turning, turning the calf;

and my father, a farmer, phoning up to ask
    what had gone wrong, he could not keep his worry
        out of his voice. Perhaps I should have prayed

to him, or to some other powerful god
    assigned to *me*, when you were stalled
        inside the birth canal; and also:

when they ripped you out and cut us free.

ADAGIO

We never said aloud: into the earth or fire.
And if earth, then where. And if fire, then where

                              to cast the ashes.

Each thought the other would choose: choosing for two, not one—
the body lying flat, the body left upright.

And if a stone.

MESSENGER

I.

First I smelled it, hovering near the bed:
distinctly saline, as in a ship's wake;

a bit of dust and mold, like moth-found fur;
also something grassy, crushed herb, sharper.

After that, when they turned the ward lights out,
the space ship glowing at the nurses' hub,

his pod stilled and darkened, only the small
digitals updating on the screen,

then I could see—one "sees" in deep gloaming,
though ground-fog makes an airless, formless room—

how fully it loomed behind and larger than
the steel stalk, the sweet translucent fruit.

One doesn't notice wings when they're at rest.
One doesn't notice the scythe of the beak at rest:

opaque, like horn, or bone, knobbed at the base
but tapering, proportionate to the head.

In Quattrocento paintings, Mary's face
is mirrored by the messenger's radiant face:

that's meant to comfort—*see, they're just like us.*
No, they're not like us. This had no face,

and its posture was a suspect courtesy,
stolen from a courtier who nods

to the aging king, head bowed, and holds aside,
lowered, but unsheathed, the sword.

2.

Except in wired emergencies, the signals
  sounding for a pressure drop but not
    a fever spike, a bad white count, blood
      transfused too fast, a tube dislodged, sudden
        struggle to breathe, the opiates late again,
          always late—it was my task to harry
            the Duty-Nurse, Charge-Nurse, Intern, Attending,
              to put in the rut of their path implacable me—

the workers came and went without alarm
  and thus I could not trust them—
                  they must think it
  part of the common furniture that clutters
cardio-thoracic post-surgical wards,

but I think not: I think your father's code
  was branded somewhere on its bony leg,
    631688, the same sign
      stamped on the band clamped to the swollen wrist,
        markers for an arduous migration.
          I think it was used to hunger. I think it was waiting
            for me to leave the room.

3.

01-21-05. 0400.
Before the workers came for vital signs,
halfway through the IV bag's collapse,

the cuff tightening on his good right arm,
a little purr, a read-out click on the wall,
then a hush, no anguish from his or other pods,

I think it moved. At least I can say I heard
a faint new noise:
                    as if a great blue heron,
not nesting but next to the nest, an eye on the nest,
still as a stalk beside the water's edge,
resting on one leg, had stirred.

4.

That all this happened far away from you;
that the verb "think" is stupid and unworthy;
that when all this began, the world went away;
that what we thought the world was, was a dream;
that you, the hub of that world, belong to the dream;
that you, remembered, now must be imagined;
that imagining is how we think we choose;
that the verb "choose" is stupid and unworthy;
that need, unspeakable need, is what imagines
while joy or grief, rage or terror dreams;
that there is no world except the worlds we dream;
that while I imagine you you're dreaming us;
that in the dream you dream your father rises.

5.

Birds migrate in flocks, there was no flock.

When we moved out, into the strange city,
    and I became the lone worker-bee,
        my queen—your father—fixed in the high bed,

above his heart the violent slash, cross-hatched,
    above his heart tattoos for the next aggression,
        above his heart a major vein now missing,

the oxygen-machine a lullaby,
    shush-shush, the multiple colorful pills piled
        in labeled boxes, our calendar and clock—

it didn't go back, legs dangling down like commas,
    without the soul it might have carried like lice
        below a wing, kept warm beneath its feathers:

it followed us there, and stood in the rented yard
    behind the live oaks and the oleander—
        I saw it once, I'd learned where I should look.

And when, that season ended, we came home,
    it came too. From the kitchen window, west,
        down the sledding hill to the berry-bramble,

you'd see where: in early dark, camouflaged
    among the gaunt gray alders along the brook,
        still as a stalk beside the water's edge—

of course it's there. It winters over.